The McGraw-Hill Guide to the PMP Exam

The McGraw-Hill Guide to the PMP Exam

JAMES P. LEWIS

ROBERT E. DUDLEY

McGraw-Hill

New York   Chicago   San Francisco   Lisbon   London
Madrid   Mexico City   Milan   New Delhi   San Juan
Seoul   Singapore   Sydney   Toronto

1 2 3 4 5 6 7 8 9 0 QPD/QPD 0 9 8 7 6 5

ISBN 0-07-143679-0

McGraw-Hill books are available at special quantity discounts to use as premiums and sales promotions, or for use in corporate training programs. For more information, please write to the Director of Special Sales, McGraw-Hill, Professional Publishing, 2 Penn Plaza, New York, NY 10121-2298. Or contact your local bookstore.

PMP® is a certification mark of the Project Management Institute, Inc.; PMBOK® is a trademark of the Project Management Institute, Inc.; PMI® is a service and trademark of the Project Management Institute, Inc.; all are registered in the United States and other nations.

This book is not endorsed in any way by the Project Management Institute, Inc.

Library of Congress Cataloging-in-Publication Data

Lewis, James P.
 The McGraw-Hill guide to the PMP exam / by James P. Lewis, Robert E. Dudley.
    p. cm.
 ISBN 0-07-143679-0 (pbk. : alk. paper)
 1. Project management—Certification. 2. Project management—Examinations—Study guides. I. Dudley, Robert, 1944- II. Title.
 HD69.P75L4893 2005
 658.4'04'076—dc22

2004021728

 This book is printed on recycled, acid-free paper containing a minimum of 50% recycled de-inked fiber.

Contents

Preface

Certification of individuals as Project Management Professionals, or PMPs®, may be one of the most successful programs of the 20th century. In November 2004 there were already 75,000 PMPs, and the number is increasing at an exponential rate.

The question most frequently asked is whether getting one's PMP is worth the trouble. As usual, the answer is, "It all depends." Does your current or future employer care? If not, then no, it may not be worth the trouble. However, the real question is, "How serious are you about project management as a career?" If the answer is, "Very," then certification may be worth the trouble just because of what you will learn in the process.

The only caveat is that getting the PMP primarily requires *content knowledge,* while managing projects requires *skills*, and there is a big difference between them. As is always the difficulty with theory versus practice, you will find areas of the Project Management Body of Knowledge (PMBOK®) that are at variance with practice. This is partly because people who write documents like the PMBOK are not always practitioners, but also because the document is a committee effort, and you have an almost impossible time getting consensus with a committee.

We have tried to point out these areas of variance in our book so that you can pass the test, and then go forth and practice practical skills. However, the book is primarily written to help you pass the test—which is what we're sure you want.

Collectively, Bob Dudley and Jim Lewis have about 60 years' experience in managing projects, consulting, and training. We believe you will find the book to be very helpful in passing your exam, although there is no way we can guarantee it, as test-taking is a highly individual thing. We wish you luck.

James P. Lewis
Vinton, Virginia

Robert E. Dudley
Cape Coral, Florida

Chapter 1

Introduction

PROJECT MANAGEMENT AS A PROFESSION

Project management as a profession can be an exciting and rewarding career. It does, however, take a certain mind-set to seek this profession. While many successful project managers have gotten where they are by accident, most of us who have actually sought this field have done so because we believe that there is a need for good project management, and we enjoy a sense of satisfaction when we are able to see an idea through to reality.

As a project manager, you cannot pick and choose which of the many aspects of project management to perform and which to ignore: None of them are optional! This is one of the things that differentiate project *management* from project *engineering* or any of the other support roles on a project.

You should also realize that the principles of project management are the same, no matter your industry or specialty. However, don't fall into the "A project is a project is a project!" syndrome. You will be much more successful if you actually understand the industry in which you are practicing. For example, Bob Dudley, one of the authors of this book, has 30-plus years of experience *and* a degree in construction. He would likely not be a good candidate for a software development project. He could apply all of the principles but would have very little depth of experience upon which to draw. There is an old expression, "A cobbler should stick to his lasts," which summarizes this thought well.

It is critical to your success that you have an open mind and a desire to discover where your weaknesses may lie. But you know that! It's why you bought this book.

THE PROJECT MANAGEMENT INSTITUTE

The Project Management Institute (PMI®), founded in 1969, is the largest professional organization for project managers. By the end of 2003, there were over 120,000 members of the Institute and more than 200 chapters worldwide, with 50 more in the process of becoming chartered. PMI chapters are located in 67 countries.

PMI provides educational services through their own coursework as well as an extensive network of Registered Education Providers (REPs). REPs have to undergo a rigorous application procedure that includes having their coursework certified by an active Project Management Professional (PMP®). Also, PMI sponsors Special Interest Groups (SIGs) and other forums that allow members to interact with others of similar interest.

One of PMI's best-known roles is that of Certifying Agency for project managers seeking their PMP certification. In addition to the PMP designation, PMI also has certifications for support roles and subspecialties.

PMI's Web site is www.pmi.org. It would be useful for you to visit it to see all that PMI has to offer. The entire certification process is available there.

Why Should You Get Your Certification?

There are as many answers to this question as there are project managers. Primarily, you should get your certification because you want to prove to yourself that you have the knowledge a skilled project manager requires. But there are other reasons:

▶ *Prestige.* Among project managers, the PMP designation shows that you are serious about your chosen profession.

▶ *Advancement.* A number of organizations, especially those that do many projects, consider people with certification to be serious about their careers.

▶ *Career mobility.* It is common for a project manager to change jobs a number of times during their career. If you have your certification, you are a "known entity" to future employers. They can be confident you know what you are doing.

▶ *Job security.* A growing number of firms consider certification a condition of employment. This is true as well of other disciplines—such as purchasing, human resources, and accounting, for example.

THE PROJECT MANAGEMENT BODY OF KNOWLEDGE (PMBOK®)

The Project Management Body of Knowledge (PMBOK) dates back to 1984 and was the result of a perceived need to codify those practices and principles that were common to all types of project management. It has undergone several revisions, the latest being PMBOK 2000. The major change in 2000 was the addition of a section on Professional Responsibility.

The PMBOK lays out, in its own unique fashion, the basic principles that all project managers should know. Thankfully, it has gotten more readable over the various revisions. There is, as of the time of this writing, a committee working on the next revision, although the changes are expected to be minor.

As the chapter in this book on the project management processes lays out the organization of the PMBOK, I will not go into it here.

THE PURPOSE OF THIS BOOK

If the PMBOK is so great, why did we write this book? The answer is that the PMBOK is the *framework* of PMI's view of project management, but it does not tell the complete story. This is because PMI expects project managers to have a broad and diverse background in the management and financial principles that underlie all management endeavors. You will find many questions on the exam that have no reference in the PMBOK. Rather, they presume you possess what we will call "general management skills."

This book, then, is intended to cover not only the detail in the PMBOK, but also material that has appeared on the exam in the past, as well as some of the general management and financial skills that you will be expected to have. The format follows the PMBOK outline, so that you can easily reference that document. At the end of each chapter is a summary, "Areas of Emphasis," and a sample test based on questions that are likely to be on the exam. The answers are in the appendix.

What this book is *not* is a "cram course" for the exam. We want you to *know and understand* the material about your chosen profession, not just learn enough to pass the test.

As you go through this book, keep in mind that this is but a small part of your exam preparation. This can be seen by PMI's rather detailed application criteria. You certainly need to read and reread the PMBOK, and avail yourself of some of the many excellent references in the appendix. The final chapter in the book is a review of the process and the test methodology itself, along with some hints as to what to expect on the exam.

So read this book and study the references. The last year's statistics show that 19,000 candidates got their PMP designation. However, an equal number of applicants failed to attain this goal. We want you to be in the first group! Good luck!

Chapter 2

The Project Management Context

The PMBOK contains a chapter called "The Project Management Context," the purpose of which is to outline and explain the general management skills that you need to be an effective project manager. These skills characterize effective management in any arena, and are included in this chapter as a kind of catchall. The specific skills that you need in project work are the subject of the subsequent chapters. Further, the chapter covers the phases of a project, project stakeholders, and in-depth, organizational structures and how they affect the effectiveness of your project team.

PROJECT PHASES

All projects can be thought of as series of phases that have defined beginnings and defined endpoints. While it is true that the individual phases often overlap—a process the PMBOK describes at *fast*

Fast tracking: Overlapping the phase of a project

tracking—they can be viewed as entities unto themselves. The term *project life cycle* is used to describe the agglomeration of all phases in the project.

> **Project life cycle: Collectively, all the phases of the project**

Project phases are usually considered to have an endpoint that results in some sort of *deliverable*. By this I mean that the requirements definition phase of a software project would result in a document that explained the requirements and will serve as the basis for the detailed design. Likewise, the feasibility phase of a construction project would conclude with a document that outlined the extent and depth of the study and would offer supporting evidence for the conclusion drawn.

> **Deliverable: A tangible, verifiable work product**

The purpose of the phased approach is to allow management to decide whether to proceed with a project without having to commit large amounts of resources.

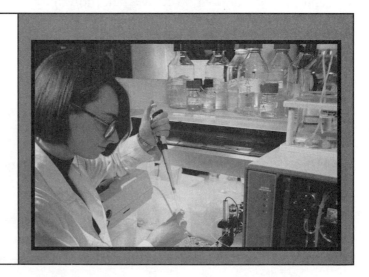

Deliverable: a tangible, verifiable work product

The phase intervals are referred to as *phase exits, stage gates,* or *kill points,* however cumbersome those phrases might be.

> **Each phase has a defined endpoint**

PROJECT LIFE CYCLES

The project life cycle covers the project from start to finish. It describes the work to be done and identifies those that are to do it throughout the various phases of the project. There are no two project life cycles identical, but there are groups of projects that share common characteristics. The PMBOK goes into great detail on three representative life cycles, so I will not elaborate on them further here. You should study the examples to understand the differences and similarities. However, there are some common characteristics of virtually all life cycles for all sorts of projects that I want to cover.

Simple projects often call for simple procedures, due to the fact that the less complex projects generally cannot support the staffing and resources needed on a more difficult one. When a project gets to the point that it needs a more detailed and stylized approach, your organization should develop a set of standard proto-

> **Project management methodology: A Structured approach to projects**

cols that more clearly regulate the way a project is run. You should not view this in a negative light. This set of procedures, called a *project management methodology,* is in place to act as a sort of paper memory to guide you through the process.

There are three elements that you should compare over the life of the project. These are cost/staffing, risk, and your ability to influence the project outcome.

A simple graph of cost/risk versus time can be used to demonstrate the degree of influence over scope and cost, and the relative risk that exists at any given time (Figure 2.1). This graph is meant to be representative, not definitive. As can be seen, the ability to influence the outcome of the project is high in the beginning and becomes more difficult (and expensive) as time passes. Likewise, the resource cost to the project starts low (few people) and rises as the project progresses, finally leveling as staff is reassigned due to a lighter workload.

Risk follows a pattern of being very high at the beginning, and dropping off as time progresses and the opportunity for problems lessens.

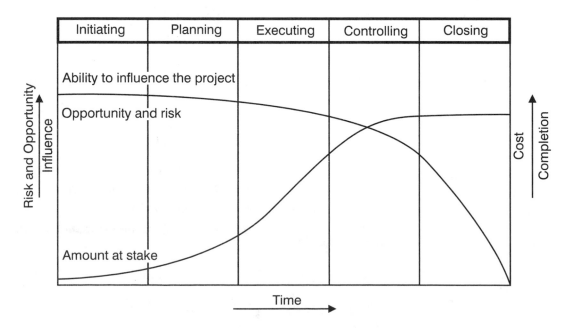

Figure 2.1   Project Life Cycle

STAKEHOLDERS

Stakeholder is a grossly overused word that has practically become trite. However, it is one of the topics in Chapter 2. Stakeholder simply means anyone influenced by or involved in the project. All projects have inside and outside stakeholders that must be considered. The

> **Stakeholder: Anyone who is actively involved in, is affected by, or is in a position to exert influence on, the project**

PMBOK describes five groups that it considers common to all projects:

- ▶ You, the project manager.

- ▶ The customers that will use the product produced by the project. These can be wide and deep, in that customers of the direct customers also need to be considered. For example, you might be building an office building for a developer (Customer A), but you need to consider the local government (Customer B), the neighboring structures (Customer C), the future tenants (Customer D), and so on.

- ▶ The performing organization. In the example above, you might work for the architect or a contractor. Either would be the performing organization.

- ▶ Other project team members that have a stake in the outcome based on employment and reputation.

- ▶ The project sponsor. Often this will be someone senior in an organization that will provide or arrange approval and funding for the project, but who does not perform any day-to-day activities.

In addition, there are any number of secondary stakeholders, depending on the nature of the project. Continuing the example above, neighboring households may have to endure noise and congestion. The media may report stories based on conjecture if they are not involved. Trade unions may have an impact on the job. They must be engaged in the process. One key point to bear in mind is that the influences and desires of the stakeholders will be varied and diverse. One of the management skills you need is to be able to develop consensus. Another is the capacity to accept decisions that may not be to your liking, or even in the project's best interest.

ORGANIZATIONS AND THEIR INFLUENCE

The structure of an organization will greatly influence how well you can perform as a project manager. Basically, organizations can be grouped as *project based* or *non-project based.*

Project-based organizations are those whose primary focus is performing projects. For example, contractors, architects, and consultants all work in a project-oriented manner. They have systems in place to handle the unique characteristics of projects, such as accounting systems and purchasing systems that are geared to the "one-time" nature of the work.

Even within non-project-based organizations there frequently exists a group that acts as an in-house engineering consultant. While the primary organization's efforts are directed at continuing operations, the project group has its own accounting and purchasing section.

Non-project-based organizations are set up to run a business on a day-to-day basis. For example, the support systems in a hospital are designed to maintain a supply of goods and services to keep the doctors and nursing staff focused on patient care, not building an addition or installing a new x-ray machine. Likewise, grocery stores need to control the flow of food to ensure customer satisfaction. Systems designed to buy canned peas do not work well when expanding the store.

You might imagine that managing a project without adequate project management systems in place can be taxing. The purchasing manager may be adept at getting the best price for raw materials, but probably does not understand buying capital equipment or consulting services. The accounting department probably runs a general ledger system and has no means to operate a cost-based system needed for projects.

Also, the cultures of the two types of organizations are likely to be quite different. Project-based groups may be more adventuresome in that they are used to dealing with the unknowns that exist at the beginning of a project. They have systems to address these, and the organizational confidence that they will be successful. Innovation and open-mindedness are rewarded.

Non-project-based organizations may be more traditional and conservative in their approach, since the business model likely contains fewer unknowns or risks. Of course, there are exceptions in both cases. You need to assess the organization's culture so that you can adapt your management style to be in harmony with it.

ORGANIZATION STRUCTURES

The PMBOK describes a range of structures that organizations can adapt. These range from *functional* to *projectized* at the extremes, with a variety of *matrix* organizations in between. Remember, the structure of an organization can greatly influence your ability to manage projects!

Functional organizations tend to be non-project based. They are characterized by a vertical hierarchy whereby activities are limited to the charter of the group. For example, the maintenance department would not have any design ability, nor would the design group have any responsibility for overseeing installations. Decisions tend to be pushed up the organization for managers to decide and communicate. Little authority exists below this level. Functional organizations are most commonly found in companies involved in ongoing operations with few if any projects. Financial institutions and insurance companies are examples.

ORGANIZATIONAL STRUCTURES

► **Functional**

► **Weak matrix**

► **Balanced matrix**

► **Strong matrix**

► **Projectized**

Projectized groups, on the other hand, are characterized by considerable authority and decision-making ability within the group assigned to manage the project. You might be in an organization that has several projects going at a time. In this case, the individual project teams would report to a manager whose role is to provide *project coordination* so that the resources available can be best used. Computer software development companies with many individual projects benefit from this type of organization.

Organizations such as engineering firms and construction companies are almost always projectized, since doing projects is their single focus.

Matrix organizations are a hybrid of these two. In a matrix setup, employees report to a functional, or administrative, manager within a functional area (such as accounting). However, when the need arises, project teams are formed across functions to manage the project. For example, in a hospital that is installing a new patient-tracking system, representatives of several departments might be assigned to implement the project. Such a team is frequently called a task force. Depending on the project, a project manager would be assigned from one of several functional groups. Some matrix organizations have a Projects functional group that draws its staff from other functional groups. The PMBOK refers to these as strong or composite organizations.

The PMBOK distinguishes between the gradations of matrix organizations.

TYPES OF MATRIX ORGANIZATIONS

Weak Matrix

In a weak matrix, the members of the project team are pulled from the various functional units in the organization. The project manager will likely be selected from these individuals, and may or may not have the requisite skills to manage a project. In addition, the individuals on the project will likely still have functional roles to play back in their home unit, which jeopardizes the project since there will be times when this causes delays and conflicts.

Balanced Matrix

A balanced matrix is a step up from the weak matrix in that one of the functional management units will assign a project manager as well as staff, to serve with the staff of other units. The key here is that the project manager is assigned full time, although other team members may be part time. Since the organization's commitment to project work is higher than in a weak matrix, the chances of success increase.

Strong Matrix

A strong matrix organization is one that dedicates a staff of full-time project managers to run projects. These project managers report to a manager who is on the same level with the functional unit managers. The distinct advantage of this organization is that all of the senior managers report to the same senior manager, thereby ensuring that the project will get appropriate attention.

Another advantage of a strong matrix is that the project support staff is full time. This is critical for such functions as document control, accounting, and purchasing. These items tend to be done poorly in weak matrix organizations.

GENERAL MANAGEMENT SKILLS

The balance of this book is going to cover specific skills that you need to develop and understand in order to successfully manage projects. However, a number of basic skills are also needed. These skills relate to managing a business or other enterprise. The PMBOK refers to these as general management skills. They include:

- ▶ Finance and accounting
- ▶ Sales and marketing
- ▶ Research and development
- ▶ Manufacturing and distribution
- ▶ Strategic, tactical, and operational planning
- ▶ Organizational structure and policies
- ▶ Managing working relationships
- ▶ Personal management techniques

Beyond these general skills, there are certain specific skills you need in order to operate in a project environment. Make sure that you understand what the PMBOK says about each of these skills:

- ▶ Leading
- ▶ Communicating
- ▶ Negotiating
- ▶ Problem solving
- ▶ Influencing the organization

Finally, you need to understand the last section in PMBOK Chapter 2, which has to do with the social, economic, and environmental aspects of performing a project. Specifically, four topics are covered:

▶ Standards and regulations

▶ The impact of doing projects on an international basis

▶ The influence of different cultures

▶ Social, economic, and environmental sustainability

CONCLUSION

Be sure to read Chapter 2 of the PMBOK carefully. This chapter—along with Chapter 1, Introduction, and Chapter 3, "Project Management Processes"—is considered very important to PMI. These three chapters form the basis for PMI's "model." The test has multiple questions on these chapters. The remaining chapters cover more "in the trenches" topics that are also taught in all project management classes. It's a good idea to study other texts for these subjects as well, to give yourself deeper background.

AREAS OF EMPHASIS IN THIS CHAPTER

The following are some of the key elements covered in this chapter and in the PMBOK:

▶ Project phases and life cycle

- Project phases: activities that result in project deliverables

- Project life cycle: a collection of project phases

- Deliverable: a tangible work product

- Phase end reviews: evaluation to determine whether to take corrective action or continue with the next phase

- Fast tracking: overlapping phases

- Life cycles define what will be done and who will do it

- Project management methodology: a structured approach to doing a project

- Review the project life cycle graph to understand the relationship between cost, risk, and influence and how they vary over time

▶ Project stakeholders

  ■ Those involved in running the project

  ■ Those affected by the project

  ■ Those that can exert influence (internal and external) over the project:

    ✓ Project manager

    ✓ Customer

    ✓ Organization doing the project

    ✓ Other project team members

    ✓ Sponsors (those that provide resources)

    ✓ Myriad other groups, both internal and external

▶ Organizational influences

    ✓ Two classes of organization

    ✓ Project based (architects, contractors, in-house design teams)

    ✓ Non-project based (manages continuing operations)

▶ Organizational structure

  ■ Describes the way in which reporting and decision making are done (who has the power!)

    ✓ Functional: vertical hierarchy, the power is at the top

    ✓ Weak matrix: the power is with the functional manager

    ✓ Balanced matrix: the power is shared between the functional manager and the project manager

    ✓ Strong matrix: the power resides with the project manager

- ✓ Projectized: the power is with the project manager
- ■ Reread the relevant section in the PMBOK to develop an understanding of the advantages and disadvantages of each organizational structure, especially as it relates to projects.

▶ General management skills

- ■ These are skills that are appropriate for managing any type of business. I recommend that you go back and reread the relevant section in both this chapter and the PMBOK to pick up some of the buzzwords.

▶ Specific management skills

- ■ These are skills needed to effectively manage projects
  - ✓ Leading
  - ✓ Communicating
  - ✓ Negotiating
  - ✓ Problem solving
  - ✓ Influencing the organization (power and politics)

▶ Social, economic, and environmental influences

- ■ Standards and regulations
- ■ The impact of internationalization: doing projects across countries and time zones
- ■ Cultural impacts: doing projects across cultural boundaries
- ■ Sustainability: recognizing that the project has impacts and influences beyond its defined scope; unintended consequences

SAMPLE QUESTIONS: CHAPTER TWO— SELECT THE *BEST* ANSWER

1. In which type of organization does a project tend to get the least attention?

   A.   Strong matrix

   B.   Weak matrix

   C.   Functional

   D.   Horizontally integrated

2. Which of the following could be considered stakeholders?

   A.   Government officials

   B.   Local citizens

   C.   The purchasing manager

   D.   Any of the above

3. What is fast tracking?

   A.   Getting approval of a project without going through channels

   B.   Conducting several phases of a project simultaneously

   C.   Applying excessive resources to finish as soon as possible

   D.   None of the above

4. Deliverables are:

   A.   A tangible, verifiable work product

   B.   Materials from suppliers

C. An estimating technique

D. A stage of the project life cycle

5. What is the project life cycle?

   A. An analysis of the viability of the project

   B. Integration of product needs into the project

   C. Collectively, all of the phases of the project

   D. A method of risk analysis

6. What is the primary purpose of a project management methodology?

   A. To free management from making decisions

   B. To guide the project team through the process of performing the project

   C. To satisfy the auditors during project closeout

   D. To specify the sort of organization should be utilized

7. What is a fundamental advantage gained by using a matrix organization in project work?

   A. More efficient communication

   B. Multiple managers to be used as resources

   C. Better use of physical facilities

   D. A matrix organization is not appropriate for project work

8. Why does risk decrease as the project progresses?

    A. Additional team members are assigned, so the workload is lighter

    B. Management pays more attention to the project

    C. Less uncertainty exists, since potential risk events have passed

    D. It doesn't; the project is just as risky until it is complete

9. In which organization type does the project manager have the most influence?

    A. Functional

    B. Strong matrix

    C. Balanced matrix

    D. Projectized

10. How does an organization's culture affect a project?

    A. Risk tolerance is different in different organizations

    B. Level of authority may be different in different organizations

    C. Management style varies in organizations

    D. All of the above represent cultural influences

11. An architectural firm typically is an example of which type of organization?

    A. Functional

    B. Projectized

    C. Vertically integrated

    D. Weak matrix

12. When should the project manager be assigned to the project?

   A. Once the budget is set

   B. During risk analysis

   C. At project inception

   D. When contracts are being let

13. What is a characteristic of non-project-based organizations?

   A. They are engaged in continuing operations

   B. They generally have a project office

   C. They typically are matrix organizations

   D. All of the above

14. Reporting and decision making in a functional organization generally:

   A. Are done across departments at all levels

   B. Are vertical in that information flows up to the manager, who then communicates across departments

   C. Are done within the project office

   D. Are the same as in matrix organizations

15. Why would a project manager need to be adept at influencing the organization?

   A. Because he generally does not have authority beyond the project

   B. Because influence dictates how things get done in a cooperative manner

   C. Because authority alone is usually not enough to get others to agree with you

   D. All of the above

16. When is the project budget set?

    A. During the initiating phase

    B. During the execution phase

    C. During the planning phase

    D. When contracts are let

17. Stakeholder differences should generally be resolved:

    A. By the government

    B. In favor of the customer

    C. By the functional manager

    D. By the project coordinator

18. How does internationalization impact a project?

    A. Costs may be different

    B. Geographic considerations require close attention

    C. Cultural and political influences need to be managed

    D. All of the above

19. Why should formal reviews be held at the end of each project phase?

    A. To determine if the project is meeting its objectives

    B. To allow the staff a chance to tend to other business

    C. To ensure that the deliverables are complete

    D. A and C above

20. The ability to influence the direction of a project is greatest:

    A. During the initiating phase

    B. During the planning phase

    C. During the execution phase

    D. During the controlling phase

Chapter 3

Project Management Processes

The chapter in the PMBOK concerning project management processes is actually an introduction to the way that the book is organized, and an explanation of the difference between processes and knowledge areas. There may be questions from this chapter, but they are generally pretty easy if you understand the structure of PMI's model of project management as detailed in the following chapters.

PROCESSES VERSUS KNOWLEDGE AREAS

This distinction is very important, so you need to fully understand it. It forms the entire backbone of the Project Management Body of Knowledge (PMBOK).

PROCESSES

A process is a series of actions that brings about a result. There are two classes of process described in the PMBOK:

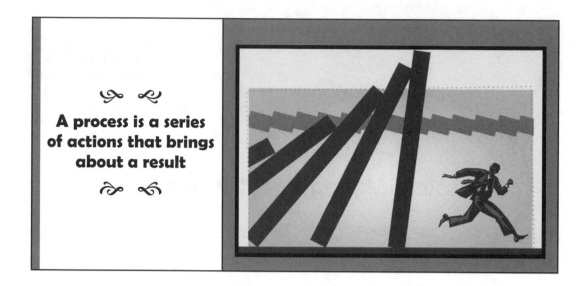

> ❧ ❧
> **A process is a series of actions that brings about a result**
> ❧ ❧

▶ Project processes, which plan, organize, and conduct the project

▶ Product processes, which plan, organize, and complete the product that the project is to produce

There are five processes defined in the PMBOK:

▶ *Initiating:* authorizing the project

▶ *Planning:* developing the policies and procedures to allow for the project to be performed

▶ *Executing:* applying labor and material to produce the desired result

▶ *Controlling:* monitoring the variables to ensure that they are within limits, and correcting those that are not

▶ *Closing:* formal acceptance of the results of the project and documenting what happened

Everything that happens in a project falls into one or more of these processes. PMI further breaks these processes down into two subprocesses:

- *Core processes.* These are processes that must be done the same on virtually any project. Scopes must be written before activities can be identified in the work breakdown structure (WBS)— more on this later. Activities must be sequenced before their durations can be estimated. Durations are necessary for costs to be estimated.

- *Facilitating processes.* These are processes that do not have to be done in any particular order, but rather will be done if the need arises. If you are assigned a project that does not need to obtain any resources, and you are the only one assigned to it, procurement and human resources are pretty much done!

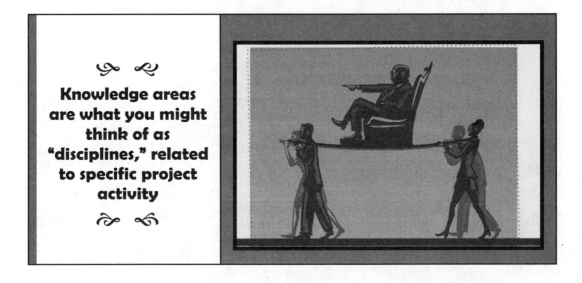

Knowledge areas are what you might think of as "disciplines," related to specific project activity

The PMBOK contains several detailed graphics that illustrate these two subprocesses.

Because the core planning processes are so important, PMI maintains that they must be sequenced in a definite order. This is the only process for which they make this distinction. Memorize the following order:

▶ Scope planning

▶ Scope definition

▶ Activity definition

▶ Activity sequencing

▶ Activity duration estimating

▶ Schedule development

▶ Risk management planning

▶ Resource planning

▶ Cost estimating

▶ Cost budgeting

▶ Project plan development

Core Planning Processes

Most of these are pretty obvious, but others could realistically be in different order. *Answer any questions per PMI.* Also note that these processes can be customized to respond to peculiar or changing circumstances.

KNOWLEDGE AREAS

You might think of knowledge areas as "disciplines." They are topics related to specific project activity. There are nine knowledge areas in the PMBOK:

▶ Project integration management

▶ Project scope management

▶ Project time management

▶ Project cost management

▶ Project quality management

▶ Project human resources management

▶ Project communications management

▶ Project risk management

▶ Project procurement management

As you can see, the knowledge areas are more "nuts and bolts" in nature in that they explain how things are done.

Keep in mind that the entire project management evolution involves interactions among all of the processes and knowledge areas. A change in one will almost certainly create a change in others. This interaction is often referred to as the "triple constraint."

THE TRIPLE CONSTRAINT

There is a model for project interaction that displays the three primary elements of a project—scope, cost, and schedule—in a triangle. The model holds that you can dictate two of the three; the third will be determined by the relationship of the other two (Figure 3-1).

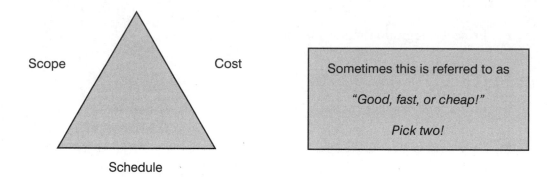

Figure 3.1

Also, there is no distinct line between the five processes. Planning may be taking part in one segment of the project, while execution could be going on in another, while a third may already be closed. PMI refers to these as "process interactions," and describes this by the following nomenclature that is used throughout the PMBOK:

▶ *Inputs:* documents and other items that will be acted upon in developing the topic

▶ *Tools and techniques:* methods and mechanisms that will be used on the inputs to produce the desired output

▶ *Outputs:* documents and other items that will be acted upon in further phases of the project

These terms will become much more familiar as you go through the course and the PMBOK.

Finally, recognize that certain of the knowledge areas are considered unique to a given process. See PMBOK page 38, "Mapping the Project Management Processes." This is a rather involved diagram—and is copyrighted by PMI—so I am not going to reproduce it here. Most of the map is pretty obvious; for instance, "Cost Control" is in the controlling process, and "Information Distribution" is in the executing process.

CONCLUSION

This chapter is important in that it sets the stage for the rest of this study. You should memorize the names of the processes and knowledge areas and the order of the core planning processes. Other than that, the exam questions should not be too difficult.

AREAS OF EMPHASIS IN THIS CHAPTER

The following are some of the key elements covered in this chapter and in the PMBOK:

- ▶ Project processes
  - Initiating
  - Planning
  - Executing
  - Controlling
  - Closing
- ▶ Knowledge areas
  - Integration
  - Scope

- Time

- Cost

- Quality

- Human resources

- Communications

- Risk

- Procurement

▶ Core processes versus facilitating processes

▶ The order of the core planning processes

▶ The inputs/tools and techniques/outputs model for developing

projects

SAMPLE QUESTIONS: CHAPTER 3—SELECT THE *BEST* ANSWER

1. What is a core process?

    A. One that is done on all projects

    B. One that is only done in the planning process

    C. Optional, depending on the project

    D. Part of the controlling process

2. Which of the following is not a knowledge area?

    A. Cost management

    B. Professional responsibility

    C. Procurement management

    D. Scope management

3. Work that plans, organizes, and conducts the project is called:

    A. Product process

    B. Project process

    C. Controlling process

    D. Planning process

4. The two subprocesses are:

    A. Planning and controlling

    B. Executing and closing

    C. Core and facilitating

    D. Core and controlling

5. "Monitoring the variables to ensure that they are within limits, and correcting those that are not" describes which of the processes or knowledge areas?

   A. Quality management

   B. Executing

   C. Planning

   D. Controlling

6. The model that holds that you can pick any two of the three project factors (scope, schedule, and cost) but must accept the third is called:

   A. Mapping the project management processes

   B. Knowledge areas

   C. The project control model

   D. The triple constraint

7. "A series of actions that brings about a result" is the definition of:

   A. A project

   B. A process

   C. A knowledge area

   D. A plan

8. Which of the processes does PMI suggest is the most important?

   A. Planning

   B. Executing

C. Controlling

D. They don't say

9. In the planning processes, which is the correct order for the core processes?

    A. Schedule development, activity definition, activity sequencing, activity definition

    B. Scope definition, scope planning, activity definition, activity sequencing

    C. Scope planning, scope definition, activity definition, activity sequencing

    D. Schedule development, resource planning, cost budgeting, cost estimating

10. A diagram that shows the usual location of knowledge areas within the processes is called?

    A. A knowledge area reference diagram

    B. A project management process matrix

    C. A knowledge area map

    D. A project management process map

Chapter 4

Project Integration Management

The PMBOK chapter on Integration Management is somewhat brief and superficial. Usually there are only a couple of test questions on this topic, and they tend to be pretty easy. Most will be situational. See Chapter 14 for more information on exam-type questions.

Essentially, this chapter covers these topics:

▶ Project plan development

▶ Project plan execution

▶ Integrated change control

It is also full of the "PMIisms" that are common throughout the PMBOK. The following item from Chapter Fourteen describes this well:

Remember other PMIisms, such as: historical information; a WBS must be used for everything; no gold plating; project managers wear white hats; and must seek out the

PMI loves these concepts

> **Since you probably don't have a job description, make one up so others will know what you expect of them**

truth and not be passive; everyone must be involved in decisions; stakeholders rule; and other recurring themes from the PMBOK."

Integration is primarily the project manager's role. Think of the project manager as the quarterback for a football team. You have to make sure that *everyone* performs their role. As you saw in Chapter 2, your ability to pull this off depends in great part on the type of organization that you work within and your general management skills. It is wise for you to generate a job description for your role and share it with anyone that you think may have an interest in or impact upon your ability to complete the job you are assigned. This is valuable because it lets you and others know the project needs and limits.

You might think of integration as pulling together all aspects of the project—such as scope, schedule, cost, organization, etc.—but it is deeper and broader than that. You need to ensure that other considerations are taken into account as well. For instance:

▶ The *product* and the *project* are linked together so closely that they should be thought of as one. Changes to one always affect the other.

▶ You need to take into account the needs and wants of the rest of your organization.

■ Operations may want the result of your project, but they sure don't want the disruption and aggravation that comes with it

- Maintenance may be asked to provide assistance that dilutes their efforts to carry out their day-to-day work

- Training will have to gear up for the rollout of new technology

- Legal will be involved in your contracts and PR efforts

- Accounting and purchasing have enough to do without your project, but still must support it

The list could go on, but you get the picture. Someone must coordinate all of these groups and activities. This is project integration, and that someone is *YOU*.

There are many other groups impacted by the project

❧ ❧

The project manager IS the integrator

❧ ❧

PMBOK mentions a couple of tools that can help you do this. Two in particular are the earned value management (EVM) system (described in detail in Chapter 7)

> **EVM and PMIS: Two valuable tools**

and the project management information system (PMIS), which is the collection of reports and databases (accounting, purchasing, etc.) that allow you to know where you stand. These may not exist as a standard system in your company, but you must get this information somehow.

PROJECT PLAN DEVELOPMENT

The development of the project plan is an iterative process in that the plan will be constantly refined and made more precise during the development stage. This stage

> **This is just the start . . . there can be much more**

is full of the PMIisms of assumptions, constraints, other planning activities, historical information, and organizational policies. You should use (or develop) your company's project planning methodology, which takes all of these elements into account. Some of the topics that need to be in the project plan include:

- ▶ The project charter
- ▶ The scope statement
- ▶ The work breakdown structure (*remember that this is a PMI favorite*)

▶ The cost estimate

▶ The schedule

▶ The risk assessment

▶ The procurement plan

▶ The staffing plan

▶ Any change control plans

▶ The communications plan

Every item in the WBS must be integrated into a control system using what PMI refers to as control account plans (CAPS). All of the CAPS taken as a whole represent the entire project. If an item is not accounted for in a CAP, it is not part of the project. You can see now why you, as the integrator, must be on top of all of these elements.

The purpose of the project plan is to:

▶ Provide a guide for execution

▶ Serve as a baseline for the change management system

▶ Act as the primary communications document

▶ Be the source of project assumptions, constraints, and alternatives

▶ Be the baseline for scope, cost, and schedule control

▶ Document the agreed-upon management reviews

There is a long list in the PMBOK that shows a way to organize and present the project plan, so I am not going to reproduce it here. You should study page 45 of the PMBOK to understand this list.

PROJECT PLAN EXECUTION

This brief section covers some of the systems that need to be in place to carry out the project. I want to emphasize two items of input that are mentioned:

> **Note the difference between preventive and corrective action.**

▶ *Preventive action.* Anything that reduces the likelihood of the consequences of project risk events.

▶ *Corrective action.* Anything that is done to bring the project back on track after an departure from the plan.

Some of the discrete tools that are mentioned include:

▶ *General management skills.* Reread Chapter 2 to understand what these are.

ৎ ৯
It is good to know something about the operation!
ৎ ৯

▶ *Product skills and knowledge.* You really need to understand what the project is providing to the organization. While it is appealing to be able to say a "project is a project is a project" the simple fact of the matter is that an ignorant project team will have a hard time being successful.

▶ *The work authorization system.* This is any system that can be used to control the work based on the chart of accounts or control account plan.

▶ The PMIS described earlier.

▶ The various change control plans that you will develop.

▶ Status meetings and other communications techniques.

INTEGRATED CHANGE CONTROL

The integrated change control system has three elements:

▶ Influencing the factors that may generate a change to ensure that the change is agreed upon. This involves using the project plan to identify the project baseline

> **You probably want to memorize this concept . . . you will likely see it again!**

so that those desiring the change can understand why it is not in the original plan.

▶ Determining that a change has occurred. You will use your PMIS and EVM systems and others to identify a deviation from the plan, scope, cost, and schedule.

▶ Once a change has occurred or been approved, you must manage it like any other scope item. You need money and time to execute it, and it must be included in a revised WBS if it is significant.

Later in this book you will learn a lot about change management plans, and how to develop them for use on your project. Many organizations use a system whereby an independent manager or board must approve changes. This keeps you from having to be the bad guy when turning down changes. It is a common expression that change orders are your friend, because they authorize you to spend money to do work that is outside of your authority!

Configuration management is any documented, systematic method used to control changes. The PMBOK definition is much more detailed, and you should understand it in this context.

> **Remember, configuration management is not just for software**

LESSONS LEARNED

You will see the term "lessons learned" throughout the PMBOK. It is generally the last item in a chapter, but this topic is much more important than the treatment by PMI would suggest. I recommend a highly formal and structured lessons learned protocol that involves not only generating the financials from the PMIS, but also holding structured interviews with everyone involved in the project—team members, customers, management, other departments, as well as every supplier, contrac-

❦ ❦

**Lessons
learned
should be very
thorough**

❦ ❦

tor, vendor, or engineer. Anyone who was involved with or impacted by the project deserves a chance to have a say.

You should critically review each and every drawing, sketch, codebook, requirements documentation, specifications, and any other work plan that you used during the project. Ideally, you should generate a detailed lessons learned document and convene the team to review it line by line. It may sound like a lot of work, but it will prove invaluable for future projects.

CONCLUSION

The remainder of this book builds on the concepts that we have put forth in the first four chapters. I think that you would find it worthwhile to reread these first few chapters occasionally as you go through the book. To many of you these concepts may be a little foreign, and a review periodically will help cement them in your mind.

AREAS OF EMPHASIS IN THIS CHAPTER

The following are some of the key elements covered in this chapter and in the PMBOK:

▶ The key elements:

- Project plan development

- Project plan execution

- Integrated change control

▶ Integration is *primarily* the role of the project manager

▶ You must understand the product as well as the project, and understand that other groups may be affected

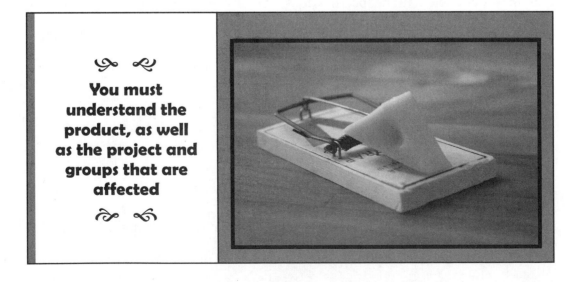

You must understand the product, as well as the project and groups that are affected

▶ The elements of the project plan

▶ The purpose of the project plan

▶ Preventive action versus corrective action

▶ Project plan tools

▶ Three elements of integrated change control:

  ▪ Influencing the factors that may generate change

  ▪ Determining that a change has occurred

  ▪ Managing any changes that occur

▶ The definition of *configuration management*

▶ Lessons learned process

SAMPLE QUESTIONS: CHAPTER 4—SELECT THE *BEST* ANSWER

1. PMI emphasizes historical records. What might they be used for?

   A. Planning

   B. Risk

   C. Estimating

   D. All of the above

2. Who is primarily responsible for project integration?

   A. The project sponsor

   B. The project manager

   C. The project engineer

   D. The change review board

3. A detailed review of the project documents, results, and plans is called:

   A. Project integration

   B. Project status meeting

   C. Lessons learned

   D. Management update

4. Who is ultimately responsible for deciding if a change is necessary?

   A. The project manager

   B. The project engineer

   C. Management

   D. The customer

5. A system that categorizes each element of the WBS and controls it according to the chart of accounts is:
   A. A work authorization system
   B. A procurement plan
   C. The project plan
   D. The accounting plan

6. For the project integration effort to be effective, which of the following is needed?
   A. Communications with all interested parties
   B. A procurement plan
   C. An accounting plan
   D. A lessons learned

7. Working to avoid an event from occurring is known as:
   A. Corrective action
   B. Risk quantification
   C. Preventive action
   D. Transference

8. You discover a change that will make the product work better and be more valuable. What should your action be?
   A. Institute the change
   B. Notify management
   C. Convene the change control board
   D. Ask the customer for guidance

9. What is the purpose of a lessons learned?

   A. Document the project results to calculate bonus payments

   B. Document the project results to assign blame for failure

   C. Document the project results for use on future projects

   D. Document the project results for the Internal Revenue Service

10. You customer is continually asking for changes. What should be your response?

    A. Do them; after all, the customer is paying the bills

    B. Discuss the situation with your management and ask for guidance

    C. Reread the project plan to see if the ideas actually do benefit the project

    D. Have a technical specialist talk to the customer

11. Giving the customer attributes beyond the specification is called ____ by PMI:

    A. Good business

    B. Featherbedding

    C. Gold plating

    D. Silver lining

12. You are near the end of the project and find that you still have $20,000 left in the budget. What should be your course of action?

    A. Notify management so they can reallocate the funds

    B. Notify the customer so they can plan how to spend it

    C. Have the accounting department redo the forecast so the money is not obvious

    D. Throw an "end-of-project" party for the team

13. Which of the following best describes the proper role of the project manager as related to changes?

    A. Record the changes as they occur

    B. Estimate the time and cost impact of the changes

    C. Work to prevent changes

    D. Notify management about changes

14. Beyond the need for project skills, an effective project manager should have:

    A. A good speaking voice

    B. Detailed accounting knowledge

    C. In-depth technical skills

    D. General management skills

15. You have just joined a new company as a project manager and have been assigned a project in a field with which you are not familiar. Which of the following would be the best to rely on during the planning of the project?

    A. Your PMP training

    B. Historical records

    C. The person in the next cubicle

    D. The organization chart

16. What does PMIS stand for?

    A. Project management integration system

    B. Product management information system

    C. Procurement management information system

    D. Project management information system

17. Which of the following is *not* part of a project plan?

    A. Lessons learned

    B. WBS

    C. Procurement plan

    D. Change control plans

18. A tool to integrate the scope, schedule, and resources, and to measure and report performance throughout the project, is called:

    A. Project performance index (PPI)

    B. Project management index (PMI)

    C. Earned value management (EVM)

    D. Earned value index (EVI)

19. You discover during the planning process that the WBS is incomplete. What would be your appropriate course of action?

    A. Ignore the problem if the omission is small; it can be funded out of contingency

    B. Complain to your management that you need an extension on the schedule

     C.   Handle it thorough the change order process

     D.   Continue defining the elements of the WBS until it is complete

20. Which is the most effective way to avoid changes during the project?

     A.   Rigidly refuse to discuss changes

     B.   Involve all stakeholders in the integration process

     C.   Estimate extra contingency funds and time to absorb changes

     D.   Use the PMIS

Chapter 5

Scope Management

Scope management is one of your primary functions as a project manager. The importance of doing this correctly and thoroughly cannot be overemphasized. At its core, scope management can be characterized by the following two statements:

Includes *all* of the work necessary to complete the project

Includes *only* the work necessary to complete the project

If you remember these two statements, the scope management activity will be easier and more efficient.

PMI breaks the scope management process down into five areas, as shown below. These are initiation, scope planning, scope definition, scope verification, and scope change control.

> **Don't confuse the "product" with the "project"**

The term "scope" in this context means the project scope. This is as opposed to the product scope. The product scope is a series of statements and exhibits that

Scope management process: Initiation Scope planning Scope definition Scope verification Scope change control

define and describe the attributes of the product that the project is going to provide. It is appropriate for you to refer to the product scope in the project scope, but do not integrate it into the project scope. For example, if your project involved installing a pump, tank, controls, and piping, the flow rate and pressure would not be relevant to the scope. Obviously, they would be used to size the components, but they are not part of the project scope. Similarly, the product scope for a software package would define its functions and features. The project scope would define what code will be written, who will do it, and what other resources will be needed. Like the pump example above, the product scope will be the basis of the project scope, not a part of it.

INITIATION

Initiation is the process whereby a project is launched, or allowed to go to the next phase. Projects can be initiated for any number of reasons. Among these are: legal, technological, customer demand,

> **There are many reasons for a project**

cost savings, product improvement, or social needs (in the case of philanthropic organizations).

As alluded to above, the product description is a key input into the initiation phase. Since the reason for the project is to support the desired product, it is logical that the product description be developed before the initiation phase. The product will likely be refined over time, but the basic reason for the project will not. If the product ceases to be viable, the project will be terminated.

A product must fit the organization's strategic plan. Also, the selection criteria must be applied as soon as there is sufficient information to do so.

The PMBOK describes two basic types of selection criteria or decision models. These are similar to the qualitative and quantitative methods described in Chapter Eleven in this book. In the project selection context, these are called *benefits measurement methods* and *constrained optimization methods*.

▶ *Benefits measurement:* somewhat subjective methods, such as cost/benefit, scoring models,

> **Be sure to understand these two methods**

comparison methods; and other models, such as economic ones.

► *Constrained optimization:* an objective approach using linear and nonlinear programming, and other mathematical models.

Given that the project survives the initiation process, you will be given a *project charter*, a document that formally authorizes a project. The charter describes the project, presents the assumptions and the business case, and authorizes you to use the resources of the organization to obtain goods and services. In many organizations there is a formal authorization by a capital committee. The authorization document provides the funds to complete the project. Someone outside the project team provides the project charter.

At this stage, the project manager should also be identified, if they have not been involved already. In the case where a study was done to support the initiation

Constraints
are imposed
by others, while
assumptions
define your
limits on
the scope

phase, the person that conducted the study will likely become the project manager. In other cases, the organization may have one staff for the study and another for actually running the project.

> **This is the very latest that the project manager should be on board**

Finally, any constraints and assumptions that management has imposed on the project should be documented. Constraints typically involve money, but may also concern travel, hours of work, business interruptions, and the like. Assumptions are the reasons and beliefs that were used to develop and limit the parameters of the project.

SCOPE PLANNING

Scope planning involves further refining the scope from the initiation phase. During initiation, the scope is more global in nature. Often, additional study and investigation are needed to develop a scope statement that can be used to document the agreement between you and your customer.

As you develop the scope statement, you will need to further study the *product* requirements to ensure that the project will provide what is needed. You will also have to obey any constraints or assumptions that have been imposed by management or the customer.

In addition, you will probably develop alternatives to what was originally agreed to. If you do develop other schemes, you should go back through the decision models that were used during initiation so you can test the new alternatives. The cost/benefit model is probably the most common one you will use, because en-

> **Giving more than is needed is called "gold plating"**

hancements to the project must be justified on their own merits. Remember, the product should deliver what is needed to make the project a success. Include all that is needed, and only what is needed. Enhancements that do not add real value are known as gold plating. You also need to resist the pressure to include things that the customer cannot legitimately get any other way.

I was running a project to rebuild a large production machine. My customer was the superintendent of the operation. She repeatedly asked that we include new office furniture, since her operating budget was not large enough to "hide" the desks. On another occasion, she insisted on a location for a piece of equipment that involved demolishing a bathroom that needed maintenance. The project would have had to construct a new one. Once again, she had no other budget to draw on. In both cases, I gave her a blank change order, telling her that when she got it signed, I would be

> **The scope statement must be signed by you and your customer**

glad to do as she asked. Needless to say, nothing happened.

The final scope statement that you develop should be used to guide decisions throughout the project. It should be signed by you and your customer, and distributed to ensure that all involved in the project understand what is (and what is not!) to be done. Items that should be included, at a minimum, are:

▶ General overview of the project

▶ A description of the product (including production rates and efficiencies of equipment, for example)

▶ Project justification

▶ Objective success measures

▶ All specific deliverables that are to be produced

Finally, you need to develop a scope management plan. This plan must include a change management procedure. It is almost certain that changes are going to be requested. If the item is not in the scope statement, you do not have the authority to include it. I frequently tell project managers that change orders are your friend, as they authorize you to spend money that you were not previously allocated.

The PMI suggests that the scope management plan be informal and broadly framed. However, I believe that is an abrogation of your responsibility. The plan must be detailed and in writing. It also must be part of the formal project documents.

SCOPE DEFINITION

This is what most project managers think of simply as "the scope." At this stage of scope development you will "decompose" the project into smaller, more manageable units, the purpose being to allow you to work with units of the project that are more easily analyzed.

It would be very difficult to properly scope, estimate, and schedule a project to build a house at the highest level, "Build a House." However, if you break the project down into smaller units, such as carpentry, electrical, plumbing, and so on, the process can be more precise. You can start to develop detailed lists and estimates and

> **High-level estimates are risky since they are frequently done without a scope**

arrange for the various contractors to perform the work. Of course, this does not stop senior management from developing a project on the back of an envelope, but that is an organizational failing, not a project management shortcoming!

The benefits to be gained from scope definition are:

- ▶ Allows for more accurate estimates of cost, schedule, resource allocation, and dependencies
- ▶ Allows for advanced measuring and control using tools such as earned value analysis
- ▶ Provides a tool for ensuring that all interested parties understand what is being produced
- ▶ Allows for roles and responsibilities to be assigned
- ▶ Can be used to further refine the scope management plan to avoid undesirable changes

The single biggest cause of scope changes is a poorly done scope. As mentioned earlier, a proper scope contains all the work necessary to complete the project, and only the work necessary to complete the project. A good scope statement should go a bit further, however. While anything not *explicitly* in the document is *implicitly* excluded, such an approach can lead to misunderstandings and confusion. I believe a better way is to list what is *explicitly included* and what is *explicitly excluded*. You

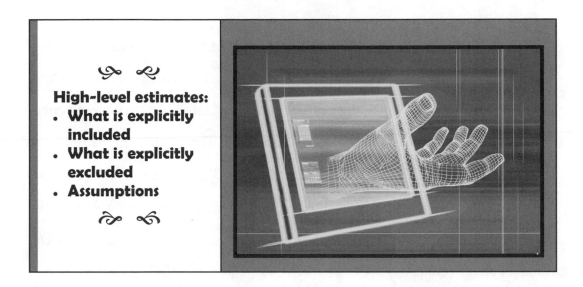

should also list your assumptions that serve as the basis of the project. In our house-building case, you might list concrete foundations as being *included*. You might specify that stucco on the foundation is *excluded*.

That the soil is able to handle the load the house will impose is an *assumption*, and the estimate and schedule will be based on this. If you find during excavation that this is not the case, then you will process a scope change. In this way, all involved in the project can understand the scope and the risks involved.

WORK BREAKDOWN STRUCTURE

The work breakdown structure (WBS) is the single most valuable tool to perform scope decomposition. There are a number of ways that the WBS can be structured, and the exact format is not as

WBS is the single most useful tool for scope decomposition

important as the discipline that you impose on the team while performing the exercise. Many organizations will have standard templates for making a WBS, but most probably do not. In fact, I would guess that most project managers in nonprojectized organizations have never developed or seen a WBS. They depend on narratives to support their estimates and schedules. This is very risky, and it is not project management. Other times a bill of material (BOM) is used. A BOM lists the major components to be provided by the project. Assigning resources and durations to a BOM is not an effective method.

PMI defines a WBS as "a deliverable-oriented grouping of project components that organizes and defines the total scope of the project." It is used as a tool to develop the project and to allow for verification and comprehension of what the project includes.

As I said before, the format is not critical, although there are several common ways to present the information. The most common way is to structure the WBS like a pyramidal organization chart. That is, the "program" is at the top, and succeeding levels are broken down into more detail. In this format there are commonly used names for the various levels. This is handy because it allows you to communicate the level of detail you expect by using these common names:

1. Program

2. Project

3. Task

4. Subtask

5. Work package

6. Level of effort

Obviously, you could have more levels on a really complex project, but these serve the purpose on many projects. You need to decompose the project down to the level-of-effort stage because this is the level where you will develop your cost estimates and schedules.

This is because you estimate effort (labor) and you schedule activities (verbs). You do not schedule nouns. PMI, however, has wrestled with this over the years, and has commissioned a study to determine whether activities belong in a WBS, or whether it should contain only deliverables. That is to say, do verbs belong in the

WBS, or just nouns? All of the examples in the 2000 PMBOK show deliverables (nouns). For exam purposes, follow the PMBOK. For running a project, I recommend that you include activities.

Figure 5.1 is an example of a WBS for building a house. I have decomposed it, as it is difficult to show all of the levels here. There can also be other items at each level.

This illustrates the graphical presentation that I mentioned earlier. The WBS could also be presented in outline form. Whichever method is used, each element must have a unique identifier assigned to it. As you can see in this example, the project, "design" has been assigned as 1. Below that, the task "structure" has been assigned 1.1. The subtask "foundation," is 1.1.1, and so on. This unique identifier can be used in the chart of accounts that will be used by accounting to assign costs to the various elements. This can also be used in scheduling software.

> **Every element of a WBS must have a unique identifier**

One common way to develop a WBS is to use Post-it Notes™ and a blank wall. You will gather your project team at the wall and begin brainstorming the project. This will take several iterations, but if it is done well, a skeleton of a WBS will be developed.

Once the WBS is complete, each item in the level-of-effort phase needs to be further documented. The term "WBS dictionary" is used to describe this documentation. The dictionary is really a collection of work authorization forms that describe:

> **Use a WBS dictionary to document your project assignments**

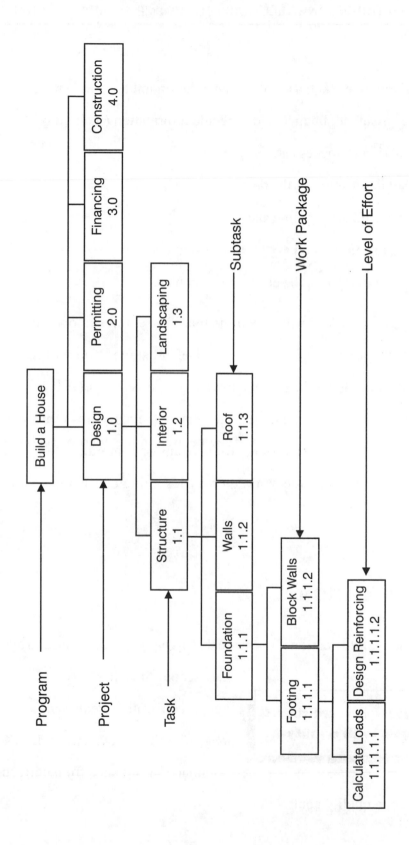

Figure 5.1 Partial WBS for Building a House

71

▶ Task information, such as project name, task number (see above), resources assigned, budget, and schedule information (including predecessors and successors)

▶ A detailed description of the task

▶ Acceptance and testing information

▶ Results of this task (such as "footing design complete")

▶ A place to sign off that the element is complete

The advantage of the WBS dictionary is that it assembles in one place all of the information about each task at the level-of-effort stage. You will recall that the purpose of decomposing the project down to the lowest level is to assure that all activities are accounted for, and that the sum of the activities represents the entire project. These forms also provide for a means of communication between you and the persons assigned the work, thereby lessening confusion about what is expected of them.

SCOPE VERIFICATION

The purpose of scope verification is to ensure that all parties understand and agree to the scope that has been developed. Scope verification deals with everyone *accepting* the scope. The PMBOK differentiates acceptance from correctness, which it considers a quality control item.

> **Acceptance goes with verification**
> **Correctness goes with quality**

Scope verification is an exercise that is done throughout the project for each deliverable in the WBS. In the hierarchy of the WBS, each element ("child") beneath a higher-level entry ("parent") must be complete for the parent to be complete. This does not mean that all parent-level activities (peers) need to be complete,

> **Children must be finished before the Parent can be considered complete**

however. In my example of building a house, all lower-level items beneath Design must be complete; however, Permitting, Financing, and Construction do not have to be finished (or even started).

You should develop a formal procedure for scope verification, and have a sign-off whereby all parties agree that the deliverable is complete. The basic process for scope verification is inspection. Inspection involves measuring, testing, and other forms of examination to ensure that the deliverable complies with what has been scoped.

SCOPE CHANGE CONTROL

It is almost a certainty that some sort of scope change is going to be requested. There are many reasons why you might be asked to modify the scope. Among these are actual errors and omissions that are required to allow the project to meet its

> **Plan for scope changes; they are inevitable**

objectives, new regulations, additional requirements discovered after the project has begun, and enhancements that will make the project more successful.

No matter what the reason, the response is the same. You need to process a scope change. This is true whether the change results in more cost, or a savings; more time, or less.

The key element of a scope change is timeliness. Unless there are overriding complications, no work should be done on the request without an approved scope change. This change should include the cost and schedule impact, an updated risk assessment, any additional (or fewer) resources that are going to be needed, and any other information that you believe is important. The appropriate level of management must sign the scope change.

Once the scope change has been approved, you need to integrate it into your project plan. I recommend that you track the cost and schedule as if the scope change were a separate project.

CONCLUSION

Once the process of developing the scope for the project has been completed, and the WBS approved, you can proceed to the next steps in the project. Typically, these are scheduling and estimating. While these are treated as separate chapters in the PMBOK, the two are so interrelated that it is difficult for you to do either without considering the other. By this I mean that to properly estimate the cost of an activity, you need to understand the resources that will be applied and the duration that those resources will be needed. Since developing the duration necessarily comes before costing, the next chapter will cover scheduling, followed by cost management.

AREAS OF EMPHASIS IN THIS CHAPTER

The following are some of the key elements covered in this chapter and in the PMBOK:

▶ The Five Processes (memorize these and their definition)

- Initiation
- Scope planning
- Scope definition
- Scope verification
- Scope change control

▶ Product scope versus project scope

▶ The Scope must support the organization's strategic goals; you will know these if the organization supports management by objectives (MBO)

▶ Project selection methods: You don't have to know the details of these for the test, but you will need to understand the difference between them:

  ■ Benefit measurement methods: comparative approaches such as economic models—generally not hard science

  ■ Constrained optimization models: linear and nonlinear programming and other mathematical models

▶ Project charter

▶ Formal declaration of the project

  ■ Includes business case, constraints and assumptions, etc.

  ■ Gives the project manager authorization to use resources to perform the project

▶ Constraints versus assumptions

▶ Scope planning: an iterative approach that results in a document that defines the scope and provides metrics to judge success

▶ Work breakdown structure (WBS): if you remember nothing else from this chapter, you need to understand the concept and philosophy of the WBS:

  ■ Remember that currently PMI relies on deliverables versus activities, while it is more common to have activities at the level-of-effort stage

- Just because you arrange your activities in a pyramid does not necessarily mean you have a WBS.

- The WBS *must* break the project down into progressively more discrete items as you go down the pyramid

- A WBS can also be shown in outline form

- Each box (or line) down the WBS must have a unique identifier that is progressively more detailed.

▶ Decomposition: breaking the project down into manageable parts that can be estimated, have resources applied, and fit in a schedule—this is a prerequisite to developing a WBS

▶ Remember, decomposition is what you are doing: WBS is a tool to do it

▶ Scope verification: acceptance versus correctness

▶ Remember everything about scope change control; it is pretty easy and extremely important

SAMPLE QUESTIONS: CHAPTER 5—SELECT THE *BEST* ANSWER

1. Going down a level in a WBS:

    A. Results in a lesser degree of accuracy

    B. Results in a greater degree of accuracy

    C. Is only needed on projects over $1,000,000

    D. Allows the project manager to better develop the project charter

2. Who benefits from a WBS?

    A. The project manager

    B. The customer

    C. The benefit of a WBS has not been demonstrated

    D. A & B

3. A WBS dictionary does not:

    A. Designate the staff assigned

    B. Include the budget for the item

    C. Define the technical terms used in the project

    D. Identify the schedule dates for the item

4. At what stage of scope management do you develop a WBS?

    A. Initiation

    B. Verification

    C. Definition

    D. It is part of the project charter

5. What is "gold plating?"

    A. "Polishing" the project to get it down to the bare minimum

    B. Including enhancements that are not necessary to accomplish the objective of the project

    C. Part of the scope verification process

    D. Needed to keep the project on track

6. According to the PMBOK, a WBS is:

    A. "A deliverable-oriented grouping of project components that organizes and defines the total scope of the project"

    B. "A requirement on all projects over $1,000,000"

    C. "A critical factor in developing a project charter"

    D. "A function properly done by the controls group"

7. If you are approached by the customer and asked to make a change in the scope, you should:

    A. Defer the decision to your boss

    B. Make sure the customer understands the impact, and proceed if they do

    C. Inform the customer of the scope change procedure

    D. Assign a specialist to handle the change

8. Scope Verification:

    A. Should only be done at the final phase of the project

    B. Assures the "correctness" of the result

    C. Assures the "acceptance" of the result

    D. Is not really a phase of scope management

9. The project charter:

    A. Is developed by the project team

    B. Includes a detailed WBS

    C. Is required before scope initiation can begin

    D. Authorizes the project manager to use resources

10. Which of the following is an example of "constrained optimization"?

    A. Cost/benefit analysis

    B. Linear programming

    C. Decision tree analysis

    D. RPN analysis

11. What is MBO?

    A. Management by objectives

    B. A method of schedule computation

    C. *Mutual* benefit optimization

    D. *Maximum* benefit optimization

12. The scope management plan is developed:

    A. During scope change control

    B. After the WBS is complete

    C. During scope initiation

    D. During scope planning

13. Which forms the basis of the project plan?

  A. The *project* scope

  B. The *product* scope

  C. The risk analysis

  D. Scope verification

14. What is the objective of scope verification?

  A. The project team assesses the quality of work

  B. The customer accepts the phase or project

  C. The customer recognizes the quality of the work

  D. The auditors sign off on the project

15. What is the purpose of the hierarchical numbering system in a WBS?

  A. To identify the parent/child relationship

  B. To integrate the project into scheduling software

  C. It can become the basis of a chart of accounts

  D. All of the above

16. Why is a standard format for a WBS desirable?

  A. All projects can be decomposed to the same level of detail

  B. It allows effective communication concerning the WBS level you are discussing

  C. It can be used to develop a project charter

  D. It avoids wasted time developing the structure of the exercise

17. Which of the following would be found in a project charter?

    A. The business case for the project

    B. Detailed estimates

    C. Staffing plans

    D. Procurement plans

18. A senior manager external to the project should:

    A. Develop the project budget

    B. Develop the project schedule

    C. Develop the project staffing plan

    D. Develop the project charter

19. Which of the following statements about scope changes is false?

    A. Scope changes represent work not in the approved plan

    B. Scope changes should be granted if the customer wants them

    C. Work should not proceed until a scope change document has been approved

    D. Cost and schedule impacts should be included in a scope change

20. "All the work that is needed; only the work that is needed" describes:

    A. Scope management

    B. Cost management

    C. Scope planning

    D. Initiating

Chapter 6

Time Management

Time management is the set of activities that allows for the completion of the project as planned. In order to allow you to develop and maintain a schedule, several topics will be covered in this chapter.

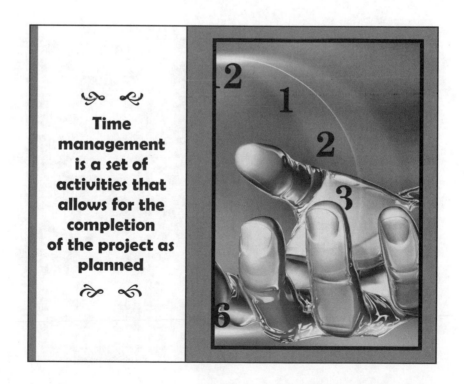

❧ ❦

Time management is a set of activities that allows for the completion of the project as planned

❧ ❦

It has been said that time is nature's way of keeping everything from happening at once, although there will be times on your project where this seems to be occurring. The simplest schedule that you can put together on a project is one where a single person does everything, and the activities can be done in any order. Unless you can truly do "two things at once," the project duration will simply be the sum of the time it takes to do each item. This would be the case if your project involved changing the oil in your car. The activities might include:

▶ Going to the auto parts store

▶ Buying the oil and filter

▶ Returning home

▶ Jacking up the car

Time is nature's way of keeping everything from happening at once

▶ Removing the filter/replacing the filter

▶ Draining the oil

▶ Replacing the drain plug

▶ Lowering the car

▶ Pouring in the new oil

▶ Cleaning up

There could be modifications to this order, but for the sake of example I am going to establish that there are not.

These are all known as *serial* activities because they all have to be done in sequence. However, if you had a friend

> **Serial: One at a time**
> **Parallel: More than one at a time**

go get the oil, you could start jacking up the car. In this way, some activities could be done in *parallel.* Unless the auto parts store was across the street, there would probably be a little waiting period, however. I will discuss this a little later.

The very basics of time management on a project can be broken down into a series of steps. These include:

> **Do things in order!**

▶ Identifying the activities that must be done.

▶ Arranging them in a logical sequence. There may be more than one.

▶ Estimating the duration of each activity.

▶ Developing a schedule that logically displays the activities, sequence, and durations. This is generally done using scheduling software.

> ▶ Monitoring, controlling, and modifying the schedule as time
>
> passes.

While it is intuitive that these steps must be taken in this order, I am amazed at how many project managers skip around and start right off with a blank MS project sheet and start filling in activities. What this chapter is going to cover is why you should not do this, and I will go over the tools and methods described in the PMBOK.

ACTIVITY DEFINITION

You will recall that I mentioned back in Chapter Five that the PMBOK and PMI maintain that the work breakdown structure (WBS) should stop at identifying the deliverables for a project. I even said that on the exam, that would be the right answer.

I also told you that most project managers do not do that, but rather continue on the level of effort and include activities. It may just be a matter of semantics, since activity definition must be done. It is just a matter of which chapter you do it in!

Assuming that you have not taken the WBS to the level-of-effort stage, you will need to do so now. Armed with the WBS, scope statement, assumptions and constraints, and PMI's favorite, historical information, you need to decompose the deliverables down into smaller, more manageable and verb-oriented sections. Recall when I say verb-oriented, I

Activity definition follows the WBS

am referring to activities, as opposed to deliverables. This is because you schedule verbs, not nouns.

If your organization has a standard WBS template, then you may also have an activity decomposition template that could be used for this section. Also, it is almost certain the WBS will be modified and expanded during activity definition. If this occurs, you need to revisit scope verification to ensure acceptance by the customer.

ACTIVITY SEQUENCING

You need to understand several techniques as regards activity sequencing. Collectively these methods are known as *network diagramming*. All are methods of graphically depicting the interrelationship between the various activities in the project. Remember, however, that this graphical representation is *not* a schedule; it is a network.

Bear in mind that when you are developing a network diagram you will be restrained by the constraints and assumptions that you used during the development of the WBS. You also have to take into account *dependencies*. Dependencies are restrictions on the order or sequence of the activities in the schedule. There are several types of dependencies:

▶ *Mandatory dependencies.* These are ones that result from the way the work must flow. They are also called *hard logic*. For example, in our oil change case, you cannot replace the filter until you remove the old one. Likewise, you cannot plant a tree before you dig the hole, or install shingles until the roof deck has been installed.

▶ *Discretionary dependencies.* These are dependencies that an organization might prefer, or that you and your team feel represent the best way to do the project. The sequence of excavation for a swimming pool might be an example. There are several ways to approach this task, and you might assign a dependency based on other work or equipment positioning. There is nothing to stop you from choosing an alternate sequence if you just want to do it this way. Be sure to document and communicate these discretionary dependencies, as they may actually have a negative impact on the schedule. This is okay as long as it is done out in the open.

▶ *External dependencies.* These fall into two classes. The first involves something outside of the project activities that restricts when you can do certain activities. For instance, the city may require that the work you need to do in the roadway be done on weekends. Public hearings may delay activities. Or maybe you can't load your software on a controls system for testing until operators have been trained.

Dependencies are usually logical—but they do not have to be logical to be real

Another type of external dependency might be that the chairman of the board wants the project to finish on his wife's birthday. They do not have to be logical to be real.

▶ *A final type of dependency is a milestone.* You may have an agreement that a certain part of the project will be complete by a certain
date to allow another party to begin their work. On a recent project,
I had to have all excavation and repaving done by a given date so
that a restaurant could reopen. There were even liquidated damages
(see the chapter on procurement for an explanation) on the contractor if they did not complete this on time. Yet the requirement to
meet the milestone made no logical sense given the proper work
sequence.

NETWORK DIAGRAMMING

Once you have described all of the activities and have accounted for dependencies, it
is time for you to develop your activity sequence. Recall that this is a graphical representation of the activities and the dependencies, not a schedule. That comes later.

There are two basic ways to draw a network diagram: activity on node
(AON), also known as precedence diagramming method (PDM), and activity on
arrow (AOA), also known as the arrow diagramming method (ADM). For some
reason, activity on node keeps getting confused with a PERT diagram because
both can be presented in a similar fashion. (In fact, MS Project 2000 has renamed
the PERT view "Network Diagramming" and designed it to be an electronic version of sticky notes on a wall. I will cover more on PERT—and sticky notes on a
wall!—later.)

Activity on Node

I want to start the discussion of network diagramming with activity on node (AON), or the precedence diagramming method (PDM). This is by far the most common method used to arrange activities in a sequence, and it is the most versatile because it allows for different types of relationships or precedence among activities.

> **Network diagramming means putting activities in sequence, and there may be more than one logical sequence**

Let me define two common terms used in network diagramming to make sure we all have the same understanding:

▶ *Predecessor:* A predecessor is an activity that occurs *before* a given task. In our oil change example, replacing the drain plug is a predecessor to lowering the car.

▶ *Successor:* A successor is an activity that *follows* a given task. In our oil change example, buying the oil and filter is a successor to going to the auto parts store.

PDM recognizes four different dependencies that activities can have with other tasks. These are:

▶ *Finish to start.* A successor cannot begin until its predecessor has finished (Figure 6.1). There may be more than one predecessor, so the F-S relationship

> **This is, by far, the most common relationship**

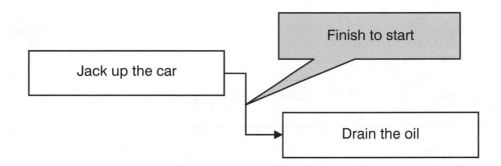

Figure 6.1 Finish to Start

would link all predecessors to the successor, and the successor could not begin until *all* of the predecessors have been completed. This is by far the most common network arrangement. Draining the oil cannot be done until jacking up the car is complete.

▶ *Finish to finish.* A successor cannot finish until the predecessor has been completed (Figure 6.2). This might be the case where your friend goes to the store and buys the oil and filter for you. In this

> **These dependencies define the relationship between activities**

case, you could start work while they are gone, but a point will come where you can do nothing more until your friend returns. For example, you could jack up the car (successor) and begin removing the filter (successor), but you would have to wait to finish this activity until returning home (predecessor) has been completed.

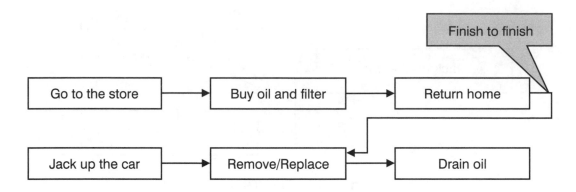

Figure 6.2   Finish to Finish

▶ *Start to start.* A successor cannot start until a predecessor has started (Figure 6.3). If your friend was helping you change the oil, he could start pouring in the new oil as soon as you began the task, replacing the drain plug. While this might seem a little risky, the actual task, pouring in the new oil, probably includes the subtasks of opening the bottles, installing a funnel, etc.

▶ *Start to finish.* A successor task cannot be completed until a predecessor task is started (Figure 6.4). This is one of the most

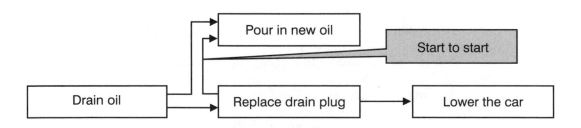

Figure 6.3   Start to Start

difficult and confusing types of relationship, and it should be
avoided. Usually, the tasks can be resorted or resources
changed to avoid
start-to-finish relation-
ships. They should only
used by professional

Avoid using start-to-finish relationships

schedulers, as unexpected results frequently occur. This is a
little easier to understand if you accept the fact that a successor
task can actually start before a predecessor task by the use of
lead-time. There is no good example in the oil change case, but
if you think about building a house using a generator until permanent power is energized, you can see that "run generator"
cannot finish until the task "energize permanent power" begins. In this case, you would schedule the running of the
generator (and paying rent on it) for a fixed period of time before you intend to have permanent power available. However,

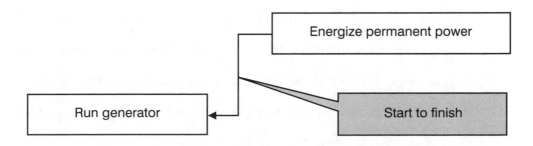

Figure 6.4.   A Start-to-Finish Network

if permanent power is delayed, you will have to run the generator longer. Another example might be that you have to maintain a detour until the main road is completed.

Once again, remember the definition for the exam, and then strive to avoid this particular relationship.

The following figure shows the activity-on-node network diagram for the oil change project. Note that I have your friend going to the store for you, hence the finish-to-finish relationship between C: Returning home, and E: Removing/replace the oil filter. Had I divided up task E into two steps, one to remove and one to replace, then this finish-to-finish relationship would not have been necessary; a finish to start between Returning home and Replacing the filter would be appropriate. The task, Removing the filter would still have to be done before Replacing the filter, but would have no relationship to Returning home.

Also, note the relationship between F: Draining the oil, G: Replacing the drain plug, and I: Pouring in the new oil. Replacing the drain plug cannot be done until the old oil has been drained (finish to start), and Pouring in the new oil cannot begin until Draining the oil is done, so there is a finish-to-start relationship there. However, you will recall that your friend is going to begin Pouring in the new oil as soon as you start Replacing the drain plug (you better hope the threads are clean!). While this is not likely, it does demonstrate a start-to-start dependency.

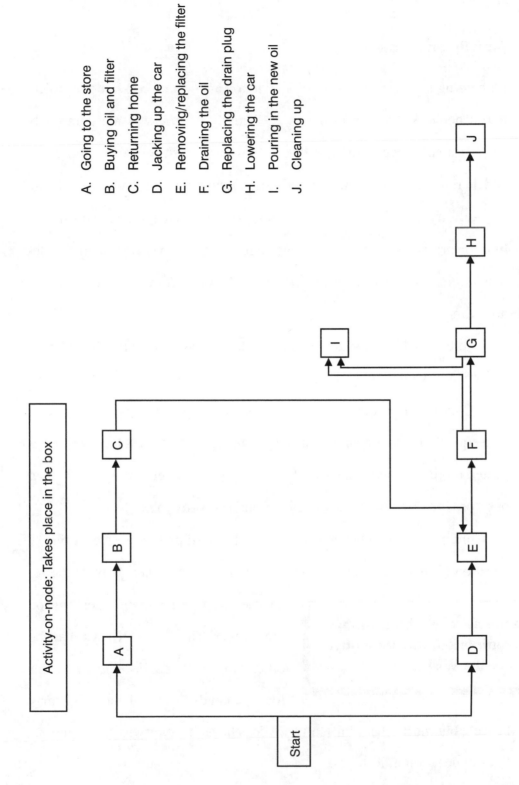

Activity-on-node: Takes place in the box

A. Going to the store
B. Buying oil and filter
C. Returning home
D. Jacking up the car
E. Removing/replacing the filter
F. Draining the oil
G. Replacing the drain plug
H. Lowering the car
I. Pouring in the new oil
J. Cleaning up

Figure 6.5 Activity-on-Node Network

95

Activity on Arrow

I am going to cover the basics of activity on arrow, and convert our project into a network diagram using AOA. Activity on arrow is not commonly used, primarily due to the fact that it only used finish-to-start relationships and therefore has to use dummy activities to show anything more complex.

Activity on arrow, as its name suggests, shows the actual tasks on the line, or arrow, and the Nodes that connect the arrows represent the dependencies. Figure 6.6 shows the oil change project in activity-on-arrow notation.

There are other ways to draw network diagrams. The PMBOK mentions Graphical Evaluation and Review Technique (GERT) as one of these. GERT allows for loops and conditional branches. Loops are iterative, nonsequential relationships that recognize that a test may have to be repeated more than once, or a specification may have to go through more than one "produce-review-revise" cycle before it is ready to publish.

Conditional Branches are "if-then" relationships that answer a binary question (Is it good or bad? Does it pass or fail?) and then provide the response (ship or rework) depending on the answer. The PMBOK says that the other two methods do not allow for loops or conditional branches. This may be true, but most scheduling software does have the ability to insert subroutines at decision milestones.

> **Once the network diagram has been completed, you may have to revise the WBS**

Note that the *dummy activity* EE had to be added to show the relationship between "Returning home" and "Removing/replacing the filter." Also, with only finish-to-start relationships, the ability to diagram the start of "Replacing the drain plug" and "Pouring in the new oil" becomes impractical.

Activity on arrow: Work takes place on the arrows, and the boxes define the relationships

A. Going to the store
B. Buying oil and filter
C. Returning home
D. Jacking up the car
E. Removing/replacing the filter
F. Draining the oil
G. Replacing the drain plug
H. Lowering the car
I. Pouring in the new oil
J. Cleaning up

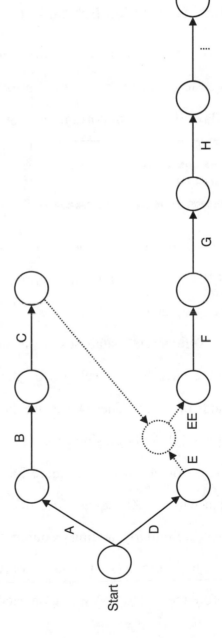

Figure 6. Activity-on-Arrow Network

The result of network diagramming is the actual network diagram itself, and feedback on the tools and inputs used to develop it. It is appropriate to revisit the WBS and other inputs and revise them as needed.

Activity Duration Estimating

In order to develop a schedule from the network diagram, you will next need to estimate the duration of each task. You also need to analyze any delays (lags) or opportunities to get an early start (leads). More on these two items later.

> **PMI loves the term "historical information"!**

A number of tools are available for estimating task duration. If the task is repetitive, records from the previous attempts can be used. This is a favorite of PMI, and they refer to it as historical information. (This will likely appear on the exam at least once.)

Commercial databases are available for many construction activities. These have been developed by measuring actual activity durations thousands of times. These tasks are then accumulated into modules, such as a square foot of brick sidewalk. The scale of the project is also taken into account; for instance, a 1-square-foot sidewalk will have a higher unit cost than will a 1,000-square-foot sidewalk due to the fixed-cost elements involved. Similarly, adding resources to a task can reduce the duration proportionally—up to a point. You can only put so many programmers on a project before they wind up waiting on each other to finish tasks.

Along these lines, by the way, it is imprudent to schedule a person eight hours a shift. Research has shown that such things as breaks, hallway conversations, phone calls, and retrieving and replacing files or tools reduces the productive day to five or six hours, at the outside. Historical information will take this into account.

Some common types of duration estimating are:

▶ *Analogous.* This is also called *top-down* estimating. It involves drawing detail from other similar projects to estimate the duration of various activities. If the projects are really similar—like building a fast food restaurant—then a high degree of accuracy can be obtained. This is a form of PMI's expert judgment and historical information.

▶ *Bottom-up.* This is where the estimator looks at the detail of each task and decides on the actual time that each will require.

ฬ ๕
**Nobody
can be productively
scheduled for an
entire 8-hour day**
๛ ๙

Bottom-up estimating is very time consuming and depends on the ability of the estimator to accurately decompose the task into its most basic elements.

▶ *Quantitatively developed estimates.* Here, you take the known quantities from the detail design and apply rates to the work that reflect the actual rates achieved in the past. For example, the number of drawings can be determined based on the engineering design. The number of man-hours required to produce each drawing can be determined from past history or estimating manuals. Therefore the total cost of drawings can be determined. This can apply to any number of unit rate items (see Chapter 12 on procurement for details about unit rate items).

▶ *Parametric estimating.* This method applies formulas and the design details to develop a cost or duration. As I mentioned before, the cost for a 1,000-square-foot sidewalk would not be 1,000 times the cost for a 1-square-foot sidewalk, due to fixed costs and efficiencies. Using parametric estimating you might discover that a machine to make 10,000 units per hour would only cost 60 percent more than one that produces 5,000 units per hour, due to the fact that twice as productive need not mean twice as costly. This is because both machines need foundations, a building space, electrical power, and the like, but one would not need *twice* as much as the other.

The result of activity duration estimating will be the actual durations,
which fall in two categories:

Duration estimates fall in two categories

▶ *Probabilistic.* This results in a probability distribution, using statistical techniques, that allows you to pick the duration that fits your
comfort level, or risk tolerance. For example, you may pick the
80th percentile for really important tasks, and drop down to the
50th percentile for routine tasks.

▶ *Deterministic.* This results in a single point duration for each task,
and is by far the more common approach to duration estimating.

DEVELOPING A SCHEDULE

Now that the tasks have all been identified, the network diagram developed to show
dependencies, and the durations decided, you are ready to develop a schedule. Before you do, however, you need to consider a couple of more inputs:

▶ *The calendar.* The working calendar obviously impacts the completion date of the project and the timing of milestones and inputs
from outside sources. Most scheduling software defaults to five
eight-hour days, with no work on weekends or holidays. This can
be easily changed in the software.

▶ *Resource constraints.* The basic scheduling algorithm assumes unlimited resources, because it was developed for construction and the

assumption is that more people are always available. Once you have entered all tasks and other relevant information into the software, you will need to analyze the likelihood of success based on your knowledge of resources. You may have to schedule around a critical person's planned absence from the project, for instance. You may also discover that you have scheduled a resource for more hours than the resource can be applied to the project.

▶ *Constraints.* These were mentioned earlier. They represent imposed dates on your project. You may not agree with them, and they may be illogical, but they must be taken into account.

▶ *Leads and lags.* These are accelerations or pauses in a schedule that you establish to make the project flow in a more logical sequence. A lead, in a FS relationship, is where a successor task is scheduled to begin a number of days before the predecessor task completes. For example, you might want to schedule operator training two weeks before a system installation is complete. This would be done using a 14-day lead, linking the start of training to the finish of system installation. If the installation slips, the training will be rescheduled as well.

A lag is a purposeful delay. A common example would be to link the start of erecting the wall framing on a building with a 5-day lag to the finish of the task of pouring the foundation. The carpenters can be rescheduled if the concrete pour is late (or early; it works both ways).

The common tools for schedule development are Critical Path Method (CPM) and Program Evaluation and Review Technique (PERT). Both methods can find the path through the schedule that has no float or slack, referred to as the critical path. Don't get confused by these terms.

Float (or slack) is the amount that a task can be delayed without impacting the project. There are two kinds of float:

> **The terms "float" and "slack" are interchangeable**

1. Free float: the amount of time a task can be delayed and not impact the successor.

2. Total float: the amount of time a task can be delayed without delaying the project completion date.

The details of each of the two scheduling models are as follows:

▶ *Critical Path Method (CPM).* CPM uses a single duration for each activity in the network. It calculates the earliest that a task can start, and the latest it must start, and compares this information to the earliest the task can finish and the latest it must finish. These calculations determine the float for the task. Tasks that have no float are on the critical path.

> **PERT is seldom used these days, but questions on the test may refer to it**

▶ *PERT.* PERT uses statistical analysis to determine the mean of a probability distribution of the various times established for a given task. Got that? It is a little easier to understand with a brief discussion of the statistics in-volved. (There have been statistical questions on the exam in the past, even though the PMBOK does not cover them and states "PERT itself is seldom used today.")

PERT Statistics 101

PERT relies on having three durations for each task. These are:

O: The most *optimistic* duration

M: The most *likely* duration (don't ask why this is not L)

P: The most *pessimistic* duration

The formula used to determine the mean for insertion into the schedule is:

Memorize these formulas

$$\frac{P+4M+O}{6}$$

For example, if you came up with these three durations:

P = 12 days

M = 7 days

O = 5 days

What would you enter in the schedule?

$$\frac{12 + 4(7) + 5}{6} = 7.5 \text{ days}$$

You can see that the PERT mean is different than the most likely, which is what you would have used in CPM. The question is, just how much better is the PERT duration than the CPM duration? As the divergence from the most likely gets larger (to one side or the other), this difference will be greater. Try the following numbers:

P = 41 days

M = 38 days

O = 12 days

$$\frac{41 + 4(38) + 12}{6} = 34 \text{ days}$$

A difference, but still not earthshaking. Plus, if you told your boss these three durations, he would probably question your intelligence. There is one other shortcoming with this system: when pressed, most people would say "X days +/– Y days." Since the difference between the P and O from M is the same, the answer will be M. Try it yourself to see why.

You can further elaborate by telling your boss that the duration is 34 days with one standard deviation of 4.8 days, using the formula for standard deviation of:

$$\frac{P - O}{6}$$

$$\frac{41 - 12}{6} = \frac{29}{6}$$

or 4.8, which means 34 days plus or minus 4.8 days.

In order to calculate the standard deviation for the entire project, you can sum the PERT means to determine the mean duration, but statistically you cannot sum the

The variance is the square of the standard deviation

standard deviations. To determine the standard deviation for the entire project, you must take the square of each standard deviation to get the variance. You then sum the variances and take the square root of this sum!

I am not going to present any more examples, but be aware that you might see questions on the test that ask for some of this detail. (PMI puts material on the test from previous versions of the PMBOK and from general knowledge.)

Other Scheduling Considerations

Other tools for developing and managing a schedule include simulations, which are computer programs that evaluate a wide range of durations for all tasks and generate statistics that allow you to make a reasoned decision. The most well known is the Monte Carlo simulation, named for the casino. It runs your project thousands of times and generates a distribution of likely durations on an S-curve. You then pick your duration based on the probability of success and your risk tolerance. (There is more on this in Chapter 11 on Risk.)

> **There are two common ways to shorten the schedule**

If you discover that the end date is unacceptable, then you need to consider one of two common duration-compression techniques, both of which increase risk:

> ▶ *Fast tracking.* Fast tracking is rearranging the network diagram so that tasks that were done sequentially are now done in paral-

lel. This may use resources to which you already have access—such as having your friend go to the auto parts store while you jack up the car. Or, it may require different resources. If you only had one programmer writing code, and you fast tracked two coding activities, you would need two programmers but for (roughly) half the time. They may or not be available.

▶ *Crashing*. Adding more resources to the critical path. This may involve more people, more hours in a day, weekend work, or more equipment, for example. It can also involve moving resources from non-critical path tasks, but be aware that this may cause the abandoned task to quietly go critical.

Bear in mind that neither technique will *always* succeed in getting the end date back on schedule.

RESOURCE LEVELING

Resource leveling is a technique for adjusting the assignment of resources. You will recall that I mentioned that most scheduling software was developed in an environment that assumed unlimited resources. By that I mean that the schedule was determined based on activity durations and the network sequence, and then the number of people needed to do the work in that time were assumed to be available.

This is not always the case. During resource allocation, you may find that a given person is scheduled for more work than is practical. You may also find that some people are underutilized. If all of your staff was equally qualified and therefore interchangeable (fungible), then you could just reassign staff. Unfortunately, plumbers don't usually make good carpenters, so you will need to use the software's resource leveling capabilities.

Resource leveling is based on *heuristics*. These are nothing more than feedback models based on trial and error, but PMI likes the word. Generally, the first option is to "level within the available slack," but if you don't have a lot of slack this may not help much. "Allocate resources to the critical path first" is another common technique. Most scheduling software lets you select whether tasks are delayed, split, or protected from leveling. Resource leveling can produce strange and unexpected results, so always work on a copy of the schedule. That way, you can revert to your original schedule and try again.

Resource leveling will likely move the end date of your project, unless you can get more resources. If the end date is critical, a technique known as reverse resource

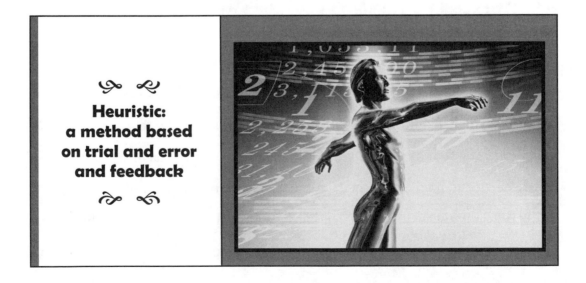

Heuristic: a method based on trial and error and feedback

leveling may be used to determine critical resource assignments, but this technique may well determine a start date that is too early or has already passed!

SCHEDULE PRESENTATION

The PMBOK describes several presentation methods and their uses. It does not go into any appreciable detail, but there have been test questions that need explanation.

> **There are various ways to present a schedule, depending on why you are doing it**

Basically, there are three ways to present a schedule. These, and their common uses, are:

▶ Network diagram: used when you want to show interdependencies among tasks.

▶ Bar chart or Gantt chart: used to track progress and report to management. They generally show dates, durations, and interdependencies.

▶ Milestone charts: these only show the start or completion of major deliverables, or key external events. Remember, a milestone is an activity with zero duration.

SCHEDULE CONTROL

Once the schedule has been established, frequent and periodic updates are needed to keep it current and to keep the project on track. The PMBOK goes into a lot of detail, most of which is obvious. One of the more important tools is variance analysis. This involves the review of each active task to determine where it stands in relation to the schedule, and using the quality method (described in Chapter 8) to detect and quantify the deviation and determine your course of action. Critical path deviations obviously require action, but many non-critical path tasks can become critical if they are not paid proper attention. There will be tasks that are so unrelated to the others that they can be done independently, and as long as they are complete by the end of the project, all is well.

The various inputs into schedule control involve the actual updated schedule itself, and any reports, change orders, and the like that might be pertinent. Delivery of equipment and task progress reporting (lines of code, yards of excavation, etc.) all need to be evaluated when updating the schedule. The impact of change orders on the schedule must be evaluated before they are approved.

Be vigilant in keeping the schedule

It is crucial to the success of your project that you be vigilant in keeping the schedule up to date. This is not most project managers' favorite thing, and it is commonly avoided in lieu of more enjoyable aspects of the job.

CONCLUSION

The logical sequence of a project includes the scope, where we developed what was to be done (see the previous chapter). Scheduling, the subject of this chapter, determines when these tasks will occur, and their durations. In the next chapter I will discuss project cost management, which covers resource estimating, budgeting, and cost control.

AREAS OF EMPHASIS IN THIS CHAPTER

The following are some of the key elements covered in this chapter and in the PMBOK:

- ▶ Serial versus parallel
- ▶ Network diagramming
  - ■ Activity on node (precedence diagramming method)
  - ■ Activity on arrow (arrow diagramming method)
- ▶ Dependencies (constraint driven)
  - ■ Mandatory
  - ■ Discretionary
  - ■ External
  - ■ Milestone

▶ Dependencies (relationship driven)

  ■ Finish-start

  ■ Finish-finish

  ■ Start-start

  ■ Start-finish (beware of this relationship!)

▶ Activity duration estimating

  ■ Analogous

  ■ Bottom-up

  ■ Quantitative

  ■ Parametric

▶ Activity duration estimating categories

  ■ Probabilistic

  ■ Deterministic

▶ Leads and lags

▶ Free float versus total float

▶ Float and slack are the same thing

▶ Schedule models

  ■ CPM

  ■ PERT

  ■ GERT

▶ PERT statistical formulas

▶ Duration compression

  ■ Fast tracking

  ■ Crashing

▶ Resource leveling

▶ Schedule presentation methods

- Network diagram

- Gantt chart

- Milestone chart

SAMPLE QUESTIONS: CHAPTER 6—SELECT THE *BEST* ANSWER

1. What two categories describe how Activity Durations are determined?

    A. Finish-start and finish-finish

    B. Probabilistic and constrained

    C. Probabilistic and deterministic

    D. Deterministic and constrained

2. Which of the following constraint types is most commonly used?

    A. Finish-finish

    B. Finish-start

    C. Start-finish

    D. Start-start

3. Activity duration is done after:

    A. The WBS is done

    B. Activity sequencing

    C. Before schedule development

    D. All of the above

4. PERT is the most commonly used scheduling method because:

    A. It is the only one that can find a critical path

    B. It is not the most commonly used method

    C. The U.S. Navy uses it

    D. It uses loops and conditional branches

5. GERT is a method of schedule development that:

    A. Uses conditional branches and loops

    B. Only uses start-finish relationships

    C. Cannot use deterministic durations

    D. Is used exclusively for management presentations

6. What is the definition of doing two or more activities at the same time?

    A. Serial

    B. Constraint

    C. PERT

    D. Parallel

7. What are mandatory dependencies?

    A. Those that are enforced by external parties

    B. Those that contain milestones

    C. Those that stem from hard logic

    D. Finish-Start relationships

8. What are the two common network diagramming methods?

    A. PERT and CPM

    B. PERT and GERT

    C. Activity on node and PDM

    D. Activity on node and activity on arrow

9. Finish-start means:

    A. An activity cannot start until another has finished

    B. An activity cannot start until another has started

    C. An activity cannot finish until another has finished

    D. An activity cannot finish until another has started

10. Which network diagramming method uses dummy activities to

    show relationships?

    A. Activity on node (AON)

    B. PDM

    C. Activity on arrow (AOA)

    D. CPM

11. What is analogous estimating?

    A. Using detail from previous similar projects

    B. The same as bottom-up estimating

    C. The term means nothing concerning estimating

    D. A subset of the GERT method

12. In statistics, the variance is:

    A. The same as the standard deviation

    B. The square of the standard deviation

    C. The square root of the standard deviation

    D. The mean of a distribution

13. What is total float?

    A. The amount that an activity can be delayed without impacting
        its successor

    B. The amount that an activity can be delayed without impacting
        its predecessor

    C. The amount that an activity can be delayed without impacting
        the project completion date

    D. The same as free slack

14. Which scheduling method relies on statistical means to derive
    durations?

    A. GERT

    B. PERT

    C. CPM

    D. All of the above

15. What is fast tracking?

    A. Applying more resources to the critical path

    B. A Monte Carlo simulation

    C. A resource-leveling algorithm

    D. Rearranging the schedule so that more activities are done in
        parallel

16. Crashing the schedule will:

    A. Result in meeting the original end date

    B. Add more resources to the critical path

    C. Prevent non-critical path activities from becoming critical

    D. Require that the WBS be revised

17. Resource leveling will:

   A. Shorten the schedule

   B. Lengthen the schedule

   C. Not impact the schedule duration

   D. There is not enough information to answer the question

18. A Gantt chart:

   A. Shows only milestones

   B. Is the same as a AOA network diagram

   C. Shows activities on a bar chart

   D. Is a method of presentation used in PERT scheduling

19. Scheduling software:

   A. Is only used for PERT

   B. Is only used for CPM

   C. Uses only finish-start relationships because it uses AON notation

   D. Can be used to find the critical path

20. Leads and Lags are:

   A. A form of precedence diagramming

   B. Accelerations and pauses used to tie activities together in a logical sequence

   C. Only used in start-start relationships

   D. Never used in finish-finish relationships

Chapter 7

Cost Management

Project estimating and cost control constitute the natural progression from Scope Management (Chapter 5) and Time Management (Chapter 6), since these three processes form the nucleus of any project management system. As such, there will be considerable interaction among these processes, and actions taken in one step will frequently cause adjustments to other areas. The cost chapter in the

PMBOK gives a very light treatment to some topics that are very important in real life, so I am going to go into more detail than PMI does.

Estimating and cost control are generally thought of as relating to the actual resources that were planned during the scheduling exercise. You will recall from Chapter 6 that resources were assigned to tasks that were identified during the development of the WBS. You will also recall that PMI maintains that going down to the level of effort is done during decomposition in the scheduling phase, but as a practical matter many project managers do this during the actual WBS development. For exam purposes, it is done during scheduling!

If you are developing a project that involves producing a tangible product, such as a manufactured item or a software package, management will use your estimate to determine the economic viability of the project. You may actually do this yourself on a relatively small project. A number of techniques can be used to do this, and I will cover them later in the chapter under "Financial Considerations." The PMBOK mentions them but does not go into any detail. You may find questions on the exam that expect you to have a basic knowledge of these tools. You will not be expected to perform the calculations, except for some very rudimentary ones.

> **Not everything is in the PMBOK**

The PMBOK also continues the theme that the basis of the project is the WBS, and therefore it should be used to develop schedules and estimates. Once these are developed, they must be used to manage time and cost together, and appropriate action must be taken when there are variances. This chapter and Chapter 10 both cover earned value management, the most common technique for achieving this. I will cover earned value management, also called earned value analysis in detail later in this chapter. When you read Chapter 10, Performance Management, I suggest that you return to this chapter for review. There will almost certainly be questions and calculations on the test. If you are not already familiar with earned value analysis, the PMBOK treatment of the subject will not help you!

RESOURCE PLANNING

Resource planning is closely related to the development of the schedule, in that you had to determine what resources you could apply to a given activity before you could estimate the duration that you entered into the schedule. For example, if you determined that one bricklayer could lay 300 bricks in a shift, and you had 9,000 bricks to lay, this would require 30 shifts. Obviously, with 1 bricklayer, this would take 30 days. Two could do it in 15, and 6 bricklayers, working 2 per shift for three shifts, could finish in 5 days. However, discounting such things as shift differential, it would still require 30 man-days, and the cost would be the same for all three scenarios. However, this example assumes that all bricklayers are equally skilled. In most cases, you will need to analyze the durations that you established in light of the skill level (and cost) for the people and equipment available in the resource pool. If you cannot get the most skilled people or the most efficient equipment, your unit cost and activity durations may change. This is another way that schedule and cost are related.

All resources are not created equal

The PMBOK describes the inputs into resource planning. You will see that there are recurring themes noted in the PMBOK, and you should keep them in mind, especially for the exam. These themes are:

▶ WBS is the basis for everything.

▶ Historical information (there it is again!).

▶ The scope statement ensures that the costs allocated will support the objectives of the project.

▶ The actual resource pool: who and what is available, and at what cost. You may need to "go outside" to get what you need, and the cost to do so may be higher than internal resources.

▶ Organizational policies and standards.

▶ Time estimates (from Chapter 6).

Once you have determined the resources and rates, and made the appropriate adjustments, you can start developing an estimate.

ESTIMATING

The same types of estimating techniques apply to cost estimating as were utilized in schedule estimating—there is little dif-ference between the two. Both aim to improve upon what is essentially a guess! To recap these tools:

> **Same types of estimates as you saw in scheduling**

- ▶ *Analogous estimating.* Also called *top-down* estimating. It involves drawing detail from other similar projects to estimate the duration of various activities. If the projects are really similar, like building a fast food restaurant, then a high degree of accuracy can be obtained. This is a form of PMI's expert judgment and historical information.

- ▶ *Bottom-up estimating.* This is where the estimator looks at the detail of each task and decides on the actual time that each will take. Bottom-up estimating is very time consuming and depends on the ability of the estimator to accurately decompose the task into its basic elements.

- ▶ *Quantitatively developed estimating.* This method takes the known quantities from the detail design and applies rates to the work that reflect the actual rates achieved in the past. This can apply to any number of unit rate items (see Chapter 12).

- ▶ *Parametric estimating.* This method applies formulas and the design details to develop a cost or duration.

Just as in time estimating, there are commercial databases and company data that will help you to determine activity costs.

ESTIMATING AND COST CATEGORIES

PMI does not cover this topic very thoroughly, but questions may still appear on the test as general knowledge.

Estimating categories relate the estimator's confidence in the accuracy of the estimate. A number of organizations establish rules for estimating accuracy, and they all have their own range of + or − that they advertise for the different types of estimate. One of the largest is the Association for the Advancement of Cost Engineering (AACE). They define five levels of estimating accuracy (range estimates are based on my experience):

> **Beware of giving out a number too quickly**

▶ *Order of magnitude.* This is usually a wild guess made to test the viability of a project without spending much time or money on it. It can range from −25% to + 75%, and numbers like +/− 50% are not uncommon.

▶ *Conceptual.* This is a little more refined, and has perhaps 10% to 20% of the engineering behind it. This may be −15% to +25%.

▶ *Preliminary.* As more engineering is done, the accuracy of the estimate may range from −10% to + 20%.

▶ *Definitive.* Once the majority of the design is complete, some say that the estimate should be in the –5% to +10% range.

▶ *Control.* Typically a control estimate is one that has been adjusted for the actual costs and quantities that are in the successful bid. Given no changes (!) the accuracy is –0% to +0%.

Be wary of these numbers! In over 35 years of running projects, I can offer two caveats that relate to the above ranges:

▶ *Order of magnitude.* You will be asked by operations how much something they want will cost, but they won't have a charge number for you to do any engineering. If you say $100,000 +/– 25%, they will immediately run to their management and say, "Engineering says it will cost $75,000!" They never hear the "+" side of the number. To give you an idea of the laxity in this type, recall that in mathematics order of magnitude is exponential. That is to say, is the answer 1, 10, 100, or 1,000?

▶ *Definitive.* It is unrealistic to expect to estimate to this degree of accuracy in most cases. This is demonstrated by the fact that bids generally come in with a wide range; therefore, by definition, the estimate was not that close. This does not mean that you should not strive for the best accuracy you can, within reason. It does mean that you should understand the reality. If a bid comes in 20 percent below your estimate you may consider yourself fortunate, but the simple fact is that your estimate was high!

> **"It is the mark of an educated mind to rest satisfied with the degree of precision that the nature of the subject admits, and not to seek exactness where only an approximation is possible."**
>
> **Aristotle (384–322 BC)**

Another area PMI treats superficially is the discussion of cost categories. These are general areas of cost that are widely misunderstood and misused. There are four types of

Covered very lightly in the PMBOK

cost that you should know. These appear on the test periodically and are covered under general knowledge, not in the PMBOK. Two of these are accounting measures, and two are estimating categories:

Accounting Terms

Fixed costs. These are costs that are *essentially* unchangeable regardless of the production rate. I say *essentially* because at some point along the production curve more fixed costs will be encountered.

Variable costs. These are costs that vary directly with production units. This is also only true to a point, because there are some costs that do not vary in a linear fashion with production rates, nor are they truly fixed.

Let's return to our bricklaying example to see how this works. Recall that we had 9,000 bricks to lay, and the rate at which a bricklayer could install them was 300 per shift. Let's assign $15 per hour as the hourly rate for the mason. Therefore, the mason makes $120 per shift and lays 300 bricks.

The variable labor cost per brick is therefore $120/300, or $.40 per brick. If the mason gets a little more (or less) efficient, this rate will differ slightly. Assuming uniformly interchangeable and efficient masons, each and every brick will cost $.40 to lay. From this perspective, how many masons and how many shifts are irrelevant to your estimate. You simply need to calculate $.40 × 9,000 to get an estimate of $3,600.

Fixed costs are a totally different thing, however. Let's establish that the bricklayer needs a foreman and some support items, such as an office trailer, truck, and portable sanitary facilities. The costs associated with these items are not variable with production. You have to pay for them whether the mason lays 1 brick or 1,000. This is where you need to analyze the work at the level of effort. One foreman can watch more than one mason on a given shift, but can only watch one shift. If you work more than one shift, you will need more than one foreman, making "supervision" a semi-fixed (or semi-variable, take your pick!) cost. You will not need more than one office trailer, nor more than one temporary toilet, making these costs truly fixed. Or are they? Recall that we had three scenarios: 30 days, 15 days, or 5 days. Since you pay for these support items by the day, it follows that the *least cost option* is to work two masons per shift three shifts a day. The variable cost, $.40, won't change, but you will save on the fixed cost since you will need then one-sixth of the time!

How does shift work fit in your schedule? You need to repeat this exercise throughout the estimating phase.

Estimating Terms

Direct costs. These are costs that are directly attributable to the installation or development of the product that is the deliverable of the project. It is commonly said that direct costs are what you leave behind when the project is over. Direct costs are the labor, materials, tools, and subcontracts needed to produce the product. Once again, things are not black and white. The tax code dictates what can be treated as direct costs versus indirect costs due to deductibility.

Indirect costs. These are costs that are incurred to support the product that the project is providing. Generally, they include profit and overhead, engineering, travel and living expenses for non-direct employees, and statutory items like Social Security (FICA), unemployment insurance (FUI and SUI), and worker's compensation. Frequently, vendor costs, training, and travel and living expenses are categorized as indirect costs. Your organization's policy on this matter should be followed

> **This is very important . . .**
> **forgetting it will break the bank**

How does this relate to the bricklaying example? The bricks, mortar, scaffolding, mortar mixers, and associated equipment are direct costs. They are all attributable directly to the production of the structure. Temporary facilities such as the truck and office trailer are indirect costs, as would be the engineering to design the project, the contractor's profit and overhead, statutory items, freight, and the like.

I am dwelling on this subject even though the PMBOK does not because it is really important that you understand this not only for the test, but so that you can produce better estimates. In many projects, it is not uncommon for indirect costs to account for 40 percent or more of the total project cost! How would you like to explain to your boss that you simply forgot them?

Another reason to understand indirect costs is that where you apply them depends upon the way you build your labor estimate. Let me explain that last statement. Labor can be estimated bare or burdened. Bare labor is the wages and salary paid to the person doing the work. In our bricklayer example, this is $15.00. However, the real cost of having the mason on the job is wages plus statutories and benefits. In many cases this is 30 percent or more of bare wages. This is referred to as burdened labor, and would be $15.00 + 30% of $15.00, or $19.50. If you are estimating on a burdened basis, you would enter this number in the direct cost portion of your estimate, and the costs represented by the 30 percent should not appear in the indirect costs section.

As an aside, estimating on a burdened basis would raise the variable labor cost of laying a brick by 30 percent, to $.52 per brick. It may also lower the fixed cost on the job, since the 30 percent would be pulled out of indirect costs, which generally represent fixed costs.

COST MANAGEMENT PLAN

As in all of the other instruments that you develop, such as scope, schedule, procurement plan, and risk analysis, you will need a plan for managing changes to the

> **This is a change management plan, just like those used in scope and schedule**

estimating and cost control document. The same discipline applies to cost that applies to the others:

▶ Have a baseline that does not change: this is what you intended to do

▶ Have a measuring plan to identify variances

▶ Develop protocols as to handle variances, such as react only when the variance is more than 5 percent because your estimating and measuring tools are no more robust than that

▶ Develop a discipline to ensure that change orders reflect the cost impact as well as the schedule, scope, and quality aspects of the product

▶ Don't make changes without prior approval

COST BUDGETING

Cost Budgeting really involves two activities:

▶ *Applying the estimate to a chart of accounts.* This is where you assign (or your accounting department assigns) an account code to each activity in the estimate. All charges for that activity will be booked to that account code, as will any purchase orders that support that activity. The chart of accounts usually forms the basis of the cost reporting exercise, and this provides feedback to the change management plan and to your estimating database.

Bear in mind that different organizations, and different groups within an organization, may have different ideas about cost reporting and when costs should be recognized. Purchasing might consider it when a purchase order is released. Accounting may not recognize it until an acknowledgment is received from a vendor. You most certainly need to recognize costs when you write a requisition, since the funds are no longer available even though they still show up in the current accounting report. It is not unusual for accounting reports to lag your activities by 60 days!

► *Developing a cash flow projection or spending baseline.* This involves applying the costs to the schedule so that your company can have the funds ready when the bills come due. Your treasurer will arrange this, since the company did not set aside all of the money for the project on day one. The trea-

> **Management needs to know when to supply cash**

surer will use accounting's figures, since this is where the actual disbursements will be made. You job is to make sure that they are aware of any changes in the timing.

COST CONTROL

Cost control involves applying the cost management plan to identify and correct any deficiencies. The system depends on an accurate and meaningful measuring system to provide the input needed to take corrective action. As I mentioned in the first part of this chapter, the most commonly used method is earned value analysis. Since the PMBOK has only a superficial treatment of the subject, I am going to provide a detailed study, plus a case study, so that you will understand the topic.

Earned Value Analysis 101

Earned value analysis is an organized, objective method used to evaluate the status of a project. It is used to assess cost and schedule performance

> **Hold on to you hat! Here comes Earned Value Analysis 101**

only. It is not a tool for examining quality directly, although quality problems such as rework can influence the cost and schedule measurements, and therefore the overall earned value calculation.

Earned value is used to provide a more credible analysis of a project's status. It was originally developed to track manufacturing processes, and has been adapted to project work. The underlying principle of earned value analysis is to measure a variable, compare it to the baseline or budget, and determine if a variance exists. A variance is nothing more than a deviation from a baseline. Once a variance is noted, a plan to handle it must be developed. In this regard, earned value analysis can be used as a tool for the quality control program for the project. This variance has nothing to do with the statistical variance described earlier in the PERT scheduling example.

I need to make the point clear that earned value analysis deals with effort. By this I mean that it is used to measure hours or the dollars expended to fund those hours. Capital goods, supplies, and subcontracts are not included. This is because these costs do not follow the flow of the project, but are paid on some predetermined schedule that is likely not compatible with the workflow. For example, if the earned value analysis were done the day before a large progress payment for equipment was made, it would look very much different from one made the day after. Also, earned value analysis can be done using direct labor only, or it can include indirect labor (overhead) depending on the accounting standards used.

In any process-monitoring system, several questions must be answered. These include:

▶ What is the actual project status?

    ■ This should be done for each module or work package in the work breakdown structure (WBS). The WBS is covered in the chapter on scope development.) These should be the smallest

> **This is the basis of any feedback-oriented control system**

practical units of work. Some suggest breaking work down into packages of 80 hours or fewer.

▶ Is the module on track for cost and schedule?

    ■ Compare where you intended to be versus where you actually are.

▶ If there is a variance from the plan, what caused it?

- This can be answered by deconstructing the module to see which of the activities planned have slipped or progressed beyond where they should be. Remember that a variance can be positive as well as negative. Both types need to be considered.

▶ If there is a variance, what should you do about it?

- During the planning stage, criteria for evaluating variances should have been developed. Be mindful of the fact that most measuring systems are not robust enough to detect a variance less that +/– 5%. It may not be worthwhile to develop a plan other than to closely monitor that particular process to forestall further deviation.

Once a variance is detected, you need to decide what to do about it. There are several approaches you can take:

▶ Ignore the variance

- This might be the case if the deviation is small. You might choose to monitor it instead.

▶ Take action to get back on track

- This could include moving resources or obtaining additional resources. Obviously, if having fewer people than planned caused the variance, there should be budget available.

▶ Change the plan or baseline

■ This is perfectly legitimate if you do it in the open. It may be

that you are running a positive variance (getting more done

than planned), and you will finish before you expected.

Perhaps this would represent an opportunity. Perhaps not.

Now that we have covered a little of the philosophy surrounding earned

value analysis, let's look at some of the measurement tools that are used.

Earned value analysis has its own set of definitions. I am going to provide a

glossary so that we will all be using the same terms. Later we will work a

case to put these terms to use. Note that PMI has renamed some of these

terms, but that this renaming has not been universally accepted in industry.

The exam questions and calculations will probably reference PMI's version,

but you should know both because old questions sometimes slip in!

Earned Value Analysis Glossary

Planned value (PV)   This represents the baseline or project plan. It is what

you intend to pay for work done in a specific time frame. This term is also

known as the **budgeted cost of work scheduled (BCWS)**. You should

know both, especially if you are using an older version of scheduling

software to perform earned value analysis. *PV (or BCWS) is not the budget*

for the entire project. This would be true only if the analysis were being done

at the end of the job.

Earned value (EV)   This represents what you *should* have paid for what

you *actually accomplished*. This is also known as **budgeted cost of work**

performed (BCWP). This is done by determining the work *actually performed* and assigning the *budgeted cost* to it.

Actual cost (AC)   This is also known as **actual cost of work performed (ACWP).** In this case, you determine what was *actually paid* for the work that was *actually performed.* Note the difference from EV (BCWP). One is using budgeted cost for the work, while the other is using actual cost for the work.

Budget at completion (BAC) This is the baseline cost that was planned for the job. It is how much you intended to pay for the *labor* part of the job.

Estimated at completion (EAC)   This is what you expect the job to cost when it is finished. This number will likely be different from the BAC once the project begins.

Estimate to complete (ETC)   At any given point in time, this is how much more will have to be spent to complete the project.

Variance at completion (VAC)   Your expected overrun or underrun when the job is through.

Remember, PMI uses PV, EV, and AC. Many others still use BCWS, BCWP, and ACWP. They are interchangeable, but you should remember both.

Using the terms defined above, earned value analysis makes use of a set of formulas and ratios to perform the analysis. These are presented below.

Earned Value Analysis Formulas

Variance plan minus actual   This can be positive or negative.

Cost variance (CV): EV – AC or (BCWP – ACWP)   A negative number means that you are over budget. A positive number means that you are under budget.

Schedule variance (SV): EV – PV or (BCWP – BCWS))   A negative number means you are behind schedule. A positive number means you are ahead of schedule.

Cost performance index (CPI): EV / AC or (BCWP / ACWP)   How many *cents* worth of work are you getting for every *dollar* spent? CPIs over 1 are favorable, and those under 1 are unfavorable. This is similar to a *spending efficiency.*

Schedule performance index (SPI): EV / PV or (BCWP / BCWS)   What is your rate of progress? SPIs over 1 are favorable, and those under 1 are unfavorable. This indicator is similar to an *activity efficiency* measurement.

Estimate at completion (EAC): BAC / CPI   This makes sense if you budgeted a certain spending efficiency but are in reality getting a different one. This calculation is simply comparing the rate at which you planned to spend to the rate at which you are actually spending. If the CPI were to be 1.00, then EAC would equal BAC.

Other variations depend on your understanding of the variance to date. The above formula suggests that the variance is typical. If you think it is not typical, then you are assuming a different efficiency for the rest of the project. In that case, a formula such as **EAC = AC + BAC − EV** would be appropriate. An alternative when you think the variance is typical is **EAC = (AC + (BAC − EV)/CPI.**

Estimate to complete (ETC): EAC − AC or (EAC − ACWP)   This formula compares your estimate of the final cost (EAC) to what you have spent to date (ACWP or AC). The difference is how many more dollars will be needed to finish.

Variance at completion (VAC): BAC − EAC)   A positive number indicates that you will come in below budget, while a negative one means an overage.

> **Memorize these tips and write them down on scratch paper as soon as you sit down for the exam!**

Before getting into the case study, let me offer some tips for remembering these formulas and what they mean.

Note that in every formula where it is used, EV or BCWP comes first. It is the first item in the variance calculations and it is the numerator (on top) in the index calculations.

- ▶ Variance formulas compare EV or BCWP minus some other term.
- ▶ Index formulas compare EV or BCWP divided by some other term.
- ▶ Cost formulas use AC or ACWP.

▶ Schedule formulas use PV or BCWS.

▶ In all cases, results that are negative (or less than 1) are bad.
Positive results are good. A CPI of 1.1 means you are getting
$1.10 worth of value for every $1.00 spent.

▶ Don't confuse EAC with ETC. The former is the final cost for
the project. The latter is how many more dollars (budgeted or
not!) you have to spend to finish from where you are right now.

Now let's put this to work in a case study.

PAINTING THE OFFICES

You have let a contract to paint four identical office suites. Each is budgeted to cost
$2,500, and each is scheduled to take one week (5 days). They will be done sequen-
tially, one after the other. Therefore the budget is $10,000, and the work should take
20 calendar days. There are several painters on the crew, so it is possible that the
work would not be done exactly as scheduled.

Bear in mind that the cost of the paint and supplies is not a part of the calculation.

At the end of the second day of the third week (project day 12 out of 20), the project looks like this:

Location	Completion Status	Cost Status
Office # 1	Complete	$2,400
Office # 2	80% complete	$2,500
Office # 3	40% complete	$1,000
Office # 4	Not yet started	$0.00

Before we get into filling out the table to do our calculations, I want you to answer two questions:

How much have we spent?

If we are at 60 percent of the time, what percent of the work have

we gotten done?

We have spent $5,900, and we have completed 55 percent of the work. Is this good, bad, or indifferent? The best way to tell is to run the numbers! To do this, you need to fill in the table below.

Table for the Earned Value Analysis Case Study

EVA Factor	Computation	Answer
PV (BCWS		
EV (BCWP)		
AC (ACWP)		
CPI		
SPI		
CV		
SV		
BAC		
EAC		
ETC		

In order to test your understanding of this exercise, fill in the table below with your interpretation of the answer.

Interpretation of the Results of the Earned Value Analysis Case Study

EVA Factor	Answer	What Does It Mean?
PV (BCWS)		
EV (BCWP)		
AC (ACWP)		
CPI		
SPI		
CV		
SV		
BAC		
EAC		
ETC		

Once you have done the tables, ask yourself: "What can I do about this situation?" You should attempt to find out what went wrong and decide on a course of action as described in the beginning of this section. In this case, you are not getting the productivity that you expected, and each hour is costing more. Perhaps there are intricacies in the job that were not budgeted. Maybe paint deliveries were late, or the paint is of low quality, requiring more time for coverage. There might have been a labor cost increase after the budget was set. The list could go on.

The most common way to *present* earned value analysis is tabular, as we have done above. This lets management zero in on those factors (CPI and SPI) that indicate efficiency.

However, when *explaining* earned value analysis, a graphical approach is often useful. Figure 7.1 shows the painting project as evaluated above.

As can be seen, the EV and AC are both below the PV. The EV being below indicates that there was not enough work done during the period. This is because this factor does not have the influence of cost. Had the AC come in below the EV, we would simply be behind schedule, but the spending rate would be okay. As it is, we are behind schedule and we are spending at too high a rate for what we are getting, much less what we planned! This shows that just because the AC is below the PV does not mean things are rosy.

Imagine if you will that there are a variety of curves that can be drawn depending on the situation. Unfortunately, we tend to dwell on the overspent and behind schedule scenarios. Remember that all variances and indices start with EV, and just because a line is below the PV does not necessarily mean it is favorable. (A more

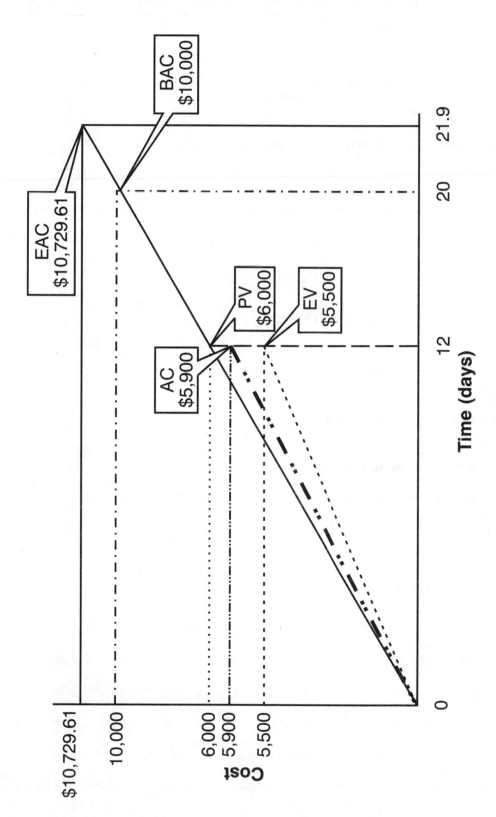

Figure 7.1   Earned Value Graphical Presentation

143

complete analysis of the various combinations can be found in texts that deal exclusively with this subject.)

Earned value is an important tool that can be used to track the financial and schedule progress of a project, and identify areas of concern so that corrective action can be taken. The analysis should be done frequently to avoid both falling behind and missing problems.

FINANCIAL CONSIDERATIONS

I mentioned early in the chapter that the exam may have some questions regarding

> **Another area that PMI tests but does not teach**

financial considerations, even though the topic is not covered in the PMBOK. I am going to outline these and give you a sense of how to interpret them. It is unlikely that there will be any calculations on the exam.

Project Justification Metrics

Several common methods are used to determine if a project is worth doing. Recall that your estimate will be an input into these calculations. Organizations generally establish *hurdle rates* for projects; if a project cannot earn at least the hurdle rate, it will not be done unless required for some other reason, such as regulatory compliance. These metrics range from the simple to the complex. The simple ones do not properly take into account the timing of expenditures and revenues, nor do they handle the change in the value of money over time.

► *Payback period.* How long will it take the revenue from the project to equal the cost? Shorter payback periods are better. If a project costs $300,000 dollars, and the annual revenue is $100,000, the payback period is three years. Of course, this assumes that all spending is done on day one and revenues also start on day one. Not too likely! Payback period should only be used to compare projects with similar cash inflow and outflow.

> **These are all methods of evaluating projects**

► *Benefit/cost ratio (BCR).* This is another crude measure that can only be used to compare really similar projects. The BCR is simply the benefits to be derived divided by the cost to obtain those benefits. It ignores the fact that the value of those benefits may decline over time. You also have to establish a time period over which you will reap those benefits. The BCR would certainly look better if you assume the benefits for 50 years versus 3! Higher BCRs are better.

► *Present value.* While this is not a stand-alone technique, you need to understand the concept in order to make sense of the next two methods. Present value simply calculates how much you need to invest at a given interest rate to have a certain amount available at a given time in the future. It is really nothing more than a compound interest calculation in reverse. There are four factors to consider:

- *Future value (FV).* This is how much you want to have at the end of the time involved.

- *Interest (i or r).* This is the interest rate *per period* that you assume will exist for the investment.

- *Number of periods (N).* This is the number of periods over which compounding will take place. Typically, this is either 12 months or 360 days instead of a year.

- *Present value (PV).* This is how much you will need at the beginning to make your goal. Do not confuse this with PMI's Planned Value (PV) in earned value analysis. Bear in mind that the PV will be lower than the FV given that the interest rate is positive.

▶ The formula for present value is not very complex, and you should know it just in case:

$$PV = \frac{FV}{(1 + r)^N}$$

As an example, what is the present value of $500,000 three years from now if the interest rate is 5 percent? Solve in months.

Future cash flows will be cheaper in dollars

$$\$500,000/(1+5\%/12)^{36} = \$430,488$$

In other words, you will need $430,488 today to have $500,000 in 36 months at 5 percent per year interest rate. This method, called discounted cash flow (DCF), recognizes what the first two do not: in an inflationary economy, future cash flows are worth less than cash flows today. Said another way, future benefits are not as valuable as the cost today to perform a project to generate them.

▶ *Net present value.* This takes the analysis one step further, subtracting the costs over time from the present value of the future income stream. Got that? What this is really saying is that the value of the dollars used to buy project resources decreases over time, just as the income stream does. In a simplistic analysis, you could assume that the costs are in constant dollars because of the relatively short time the project takes compared to the time span over which the benefits (income stream) will occur.

▶ *Internal rate of return.* The next logical step is to see if the product that the project is meant to provide can pay for the funds needed for the project. The concept of internal rate of return can be extremely complicated when the cash outlays are not uniform (they never are), and when the cash inflows are not uniform (they never are because of the learning curve). This analysis is always done by computer. There will be no examples on the exam. What you do need to understand for the exam is this definition:

■ The internal rate of return is the interest rate that makes the rate of return from the revenue of a project equal to the cost of capital plus the amount of capital needed to complete the project.

> **This is not as difficult as it sounds**

If the product can generate a 10 percent profit, and the cost of capital for the firm is 10 percent, then the internal rate of return is 10 percent. Projects that can generate a return greater than 10 percent would be accepted, and those that generate less would be rejected.

Here are a few more accounting terms that may prove useful on the exam:

▶ *Sunk costs.* Basically, these are all costs that have been incurred prior to a decision point. This is the same as not crying over spilled milk! What is past is prologue. Costs that have been incurred do not enter into the decision to continue a project. You should perform a new analysis, considering today as Day One. (The corollary to this is "Pouring money down a rat hole.")

> **Some "general knowledge" financial terms**

▶ *Working capital.* This is the money that you have available to run your business. In accounting terms it is defined as current assets minus current liabilities. If you owe more than you are worth, this will be a negative number—which is not good!

▶ *Opportunity cost.* Based on net present value (see above), this is what you give up because you did not select an alternate use for the money you are going to spend. Suppose you have your money invested at 6 percent in a money market fund. If an alternate opportunity comes along that promises a higher yield, then the opportunity cost of the new investment is 6 percent. After all of the calculations to justify the project, it still has to beat 6 percent to be viable. If it seems a little simplistic, that's because it is!

▶ *Depreciation.* One way to look at depreciation is that assets lose value over time, and you should adjust their value annually to fairly state the total value of the company. However, the only reason that depreciation exists is because of the Internal Revenue Service. It is *strictly* a taxation issue. Look at it this way. You make an investment in an asset to use in your business. You can account for it in two ways. You can *expense* it by charging off all of the cost in the first year. The IRS does not like this, for two reasons:

■ Accounting standards say that you should match income to expenses. An asset may have a revenue-generating life of 20 years; therefore, you should "pay for it" over 20 years.

- If you expense it in year one, it will drastically reduce your taxable income that year—not the goal of the IRS. Who knows what tomorrow will bring?

Or, you can *capitalize* it. This means dividing the cost

Expense versus capitalize: the IRS dilemma

by the usable life. That way you "pay for it" over a fixed period of time. One of the advantages of this is that the amount that you depreciate will be nontaxable and therefore can be invested back into the business. This is what is referred to as *non-cash cash flow* when presenting a sources and uses of funds statement.

There are a variety of depreciation methods, and the tax code is the only reliable source of current information. For exam purposes you should know the following:

- Straight line: cost divided by years
- Accelerated: cost divided by a formula that allows more write-offs in the early years

CONCLUSION

We have treated this subject exhaustively because of two reasons. First, the PMBOK treats this crucial subject lightly, but tests it as if they had covered more. (This is a fall- back to their general knowledge concept.) The second is that this is information that you ought to know not only to pass the test, but also to appear aware and intelligent in the world of project management.

AREAS OF EMPHASIS IN THIS CHAPTER

The following are some of the key elements covered in this chapter and in the PMBOK:

- ▶ Recurring theme of consistency
- ▶ Estimating tools
- ▶ Classes of estimate
  - ▪ Order of magnitude
  - ▪ Conceptual
  - ▪ Preliminary
  - ▪ Definitive
  - ▪ Control
- ▶ Accounting and estimating terms
  - ▪ Fixed costs
  - ▪ Variable costs
  - ▪ Direct costs
  - ▪ Indirect costs
  - ▪ Bare labor
  - ▪ Burdened labor
- ▶ Cost management plan (same discipline as before)
- ▶ Cost budgeting

- Chart of accounts

- Cash flow projections

▶ Earned value analysis

- Memorize definitions and formulas, and write them down as soon as you sit down for the exam

- Remember the PMI definitions

- Revisit the case questions

▶ Financial considerations

- Payback

- Benefit/cost ratio

- Present value

- Net present value

- Internal rate of return

- Sunk cost

- Working capital

- Opportunity cost

- Depreciation

- Expense versus capital and the IRS

SAMPLE QUESTIONS: CHAPTER 7—SELECT THE *BEST* ANSWER

1. Which estimating technique relies on the estimator developing detail for each activity in the WBS?

    A. Analogous

    B. Parametric

    C. Critical path

    D. Bottom-up

2. Which type of estimating technique utilizes factors to account for elements of scale?

    A. Analogous

    B. Parametric

    C. Critical path

    D. Bottom-up

3. Which type of estimate develops estimates based on similar projects?

    A. Analogous

    B. Parametric

    C. Critical path

    D. Bottom-up

4. An estimate that has a large margin of error and is usually used to test the initial viability of a project is:

    A. Definitive

    B. Conceptual

    C. Order of magnitude

    D. Preliminary

5. A cost category that does not change when units of production vary is called:

    A. Direct cost

    B. Indirect cost

    C. Fixed cost

    D. Variable cost

6. You have two projects on your desk, and can only choose one. The cost of choosing one over the other is called:

    A. Opportunity cost

    B. Direct cost

    C. Fixed cost

    D. Benefit cost ratio

7. A CPI of less than 1 means:

    A. You are ahead of schedule

    B. You are behind schedule

    C. You are getting less than you planned for each dollar spent

    D. You are getting more than you planned for each dollar spent

8. What are direct costs?

    A. Those that are fixed

    B. Those that are variable

    C. Those that involve the actual production of the product

    D. Those that can be estimated accurately

9. Present value (PV) is a financial term that represents:

    A. The current value of future cash flow

    B. The future value of present cash

    C. The same as planned value (PV)

    D. A form of analogous estimating

10. If PV = 5,000, AC = 5,500, and EV = 4,500, what is the CPI?

    A. .82

    B. 1.2

    C. −1,000

    D. 500

11. If PV = 5,000, AC = 5,500, and EV = 4,500, what is the SPI?

    A. .9

    B. 1.1

    C. 1,000

    D. −500

12. What is the EAC?

   A. How much more money it will take to finish

   B. How much has been spent to date

   C. How much, total, the project will cost

   D. The same as BAC – PV

13. Internal rate of return is:

   A. An estimating method

   B. A sophisticated project justification method

   C. A basic project justification method

   D. Part of earned value analysis

14. An SV of 1.1 means:

   A. You are ahead of schedule and overspent

   B. You are behind schedule and underspent

   C. You are ahead of schedule and overspent

   D. None of the above

15. Which of the following is *not* a consideration when deciding to continue a project?

   A. IRR

   B. EAC

   C. Sunk cost

   D. ETC

16. Working capital is:

A. Current assets plus current liabilities

B. Current assets minus current liabilities

C. Current assets divided by current liabilities

D. Current assets times current liabilities

17. What are the two ways you can treat an expenditure for tax purposes?

A. Expense and capitalize

B. Capitalize and depreciate

C. Expense and working capital

D. Sunk cost and expense

18. The two common categories of depreciation are:

A. Straight line and sunk cost

B. Accelerated and expense

C. Linear and straight line

D. Accelerated and straight line

19. Which is not an element of a change control system?

A. Monitoring

B. Analyzing

C. Estimating

D. Correcting

20. At what stage does PMI maintain that you should decompose the WBS down to the level of effort?

A. Initiating

B. Estimating

C. Scoping

D. Scheduling

Solution to the Earned Value Analysis Case Study

EVA Factor	Computation	Answer
PV (BCWS)	12 days at $500 per day	$6,000
EV (BCWP)	100% of 5 + 80% of 5 + 40% of 5 + 0% of 5	11 days at $500 = $5,500
AC (ACWP)	$2,400 + $2,500 + $1,000 + $0	$5,900
CPI	EV ($5,500) / AC ($5,900)	.932
SPI	EV ($5,500 / PV ($6,000)	.917
CV	EV ($5,500) – AC ($5,900)	–$400
SV	EV ($5,500) – PV ($6,000)	–$500
BAC	$2,500 per week × 4 weeks	$10,000
EAC	BAC ($10,000) / CPI (.932)	$10,729.61
ETC	EAC ($10,729.61) – AC ($5900)	$4,829.61

Suggested Responses to the Interpretation of the Results of the Earned Value Analysis Case Study

EVA Factor	Answer	What Does It Mean?
PV (BCWS)		You should have done $6,000 worth of work.
EV (BCWP)		The work you did do should have cost $5,500.
AC (ACWP)		The work you did really cost $5,900.
CPI		You are getting 93.2 cents worth of work for every $1 spent.
SPI		You are only making 91.7 % of the progress you should be.
CV		You are over budget by $400 *at this time.*
SV		You are behind schedule by one day, but it will get worse!
BAC		The project budget is $2,500 per week for 4 weeks, or $10,000.
EAC		It is going to require $729.61 more to finish *at this rate.*
ETC		You will need $4,829.61 to finish *at this rate.*

Note that when reading the suggested answers, the phrases *at this rate* and *at this time* keep showing up. This is because the whole purpose of the earned value analysis method is to measure, interpret, and control the project. It is not meant to be a passive exercise intended to simply report what is going on.

Chapter 8

Project Quality Management

The section on quality is typical of the PMBOK in that covers a lot of material in a brief fashion, but does not cover everything that may be on the test. Therefore, I am going to provide an

> **ISO is the new basis for quality**

overview of what is in the chapter, and then follow up with some thoughts and statistics that may appear on the exam.

PMI describes three major topics in the area of quality:

▶ Quality planning

▶ Quality assurance

▶ Quality control

A key element in the PMBOK is that all quality programs should conform to one of several ISO standards, the most common being the 9000 series and the 10000 series. ISO stands for International Organization for Standardization. The 9000 series has to do with quality management, which ISO defines as:

Quality management definition

"Meeting the customer's quality requirements, and applicable regulatory requirements, while aiming to enhance customer satisfaction, and achieve continual improvement of its performance in pursuit of these objectives."

The ISO 10000 series is a set of specialized standards that pertains to the technology disciplines. If you are not familiar with the basics of the ISO standards, you need to obtain material on this subject, not only for the test, but also because most organizations demand that their suppliers and vendors become ISO certified. A visit to the ISO Web site will be helpful.

When ISO certification became the rage in the early '90s, many companies hired

ISO started out as a paper chase

consultants to set up their systems. However, this was often viewed as a paperwork exercise, and the end result was more work for everyone in the organization with little result in improved quality. In fact, it can be said that quality actually got worse, because people were distracted by the paperwork. As the system matured, however, this became less of an issue, and the process became more streamlined.

The emphasis in the ISO standards is to develop systems and protocols for quality and stick to them. This involves periodic reviews of the systems and documentation to ensure that they are being followed. Thus, what should have been common sense became structured.

PMI also emphasizes that the project team needs to control the quality of the project and the product in a manner that ensures that both are successful. A successful project can produce a product that is inferior if the definition and requirements are not well documented in the project plan and quality management plan. It is also true that a project may fail to meet its objectives and still produce a viable product. However, what is more common is that a poorly run project produces a marginal product, if for no other reason that the project cost and/or schedule overruns impact the financial success of the product.

Let me also emphasize the difference between *quality* and *grade*. These are not the same, although they are often used interchangeably.

> **Quality and grade are not the same thing**

► Quality means that the product meets all of the standards that were set to measure the product's attributes and its ability to conform to the needs of the user.

► Grade means the product is appropriately designed and specified to meet the level of sophistication that has been defined.

As an example, General Motors makes a variety of cars that are intended to meet the needs of a varied population. This means that the cars are of different grades. The Cadillac is a significantly higher grade car that the Chevrolet. This does not mean that the Cadillac is a higher quality vehicle. As long as the two cars meet the standards that were set for their respective designs, they would both be of the same quality.

❦ ❧

**Low quality is
a problem
that you
must constantly
monitor and correct
as needed**

❧ ❦

Further, low quality is a problem that you must constantly monitor and correct as needed. Once the grade of the product has been determined and agreed to, you should not have to concern yourself with controlling it. If the software you are developing is not a full-featured product, it can be high quality but low grade. On the other hand, if you are building a mansion, poor workmanship can create low quality in a high-grade product.

You can't inspect in quality

Another attribute of a quality management system is that it should emphasize preventing problems rather catching them after the fact. It is axiomatic that you cannot inspect in quality. I will discuss this more under quality control, but the philosophy so underlies the concept of quality that I want to spend some time discussing it in this introductory section.

Prior to the quality revolution that brought in such concepts as Zero Defects and Total Quality Management (TQM), the emphasis was on inspection to ensure that defective products did not reach the consumer. When the level of rejects became excessive, management reacted by making process changes to reduce the number of rejects. This was a cost decision rather than a quality decision: rejects were simply costing too much.

The emphasis should be on making the upstream processes robust enough that the natural variation in a given process will still create a product that will meet the quality standards that were established. In an ideal quality world, there would not be inspections of either the incoming raw materials or the finished product. The real-time process control systems would prevent any defects from being produced! Obviously, we are not at that point yet, but it is still a worthy goal. However, this has to be balanced against the cost of developing processes so vigorous that they can provide this level of quality.

QUALITY PLANNING

The concept of quality planning is really fairly simple: identify the relevant quality standards and decide how to implement them in the product. This exercise must be done early and reviewed often. The level of quality that the organization desires will have a significant impact on all of the planning processes, as well as the development of the WBS, schedule, and budget. In this way, quality and grade can become intertwined. Just because your software product does not have very many features or enhancements does not mean that it is all right to produce code that is full of errors.

You need to make sure that the product and the project meet the expectations of your company's quality policy. Once this is established, the policy, and the standards that it references, will guide the rest of your decisions. These future decisions

> **Ishikawa diagrams are cause-and-effect tools**

will use a variety of techniques, such as a benefit/cost analysis, flowcharts, and cause-and-effect diagrams (also called fishbone or Ishikawa diagrams), and other tools outlined in the PMBOK. You should visit any one of a number of Web sites to gain in-depth knowledge of these techniques.

Once this exercise has been completed, you will produce a quality management plan that will define the methods to be used to guarantee that the agreed-upon level of quality will be met. You will also need to develop appropriate measurements and tools, called *metrics,* to keep track of the process.

QUALITY ASSURANCE

This can be a little confusing, since quality planning and quality assurance are often used interchangeably in industry. PMI recognizes them as separate entities, how-

> **Remember this difference**

ever. For exam purposes, think of the two in this way:

▶ *Quality planning* is deciding what level of quality and standards you will use to develop the project/product.

▶ *Quality assurance* is monitoring the quality-related activities being performed in managing the project/product to ensure that they are being done as outlined in the quality management plan. This does not involve the actual testing and monitoring of the production process, however. That is quality control.

The primary tool you will use to manage quality assurance is the quality audit. This is not among the quality control activities that I will describe later. Quality control activities are continuous, whereas audits are periodic and often random. You can perform the audits in house, with consultants, or both. *The purpose of an audit is to ascertain whether or not the methods and standards that you agreed to are being followed, and whether those methods are successful in controlling quality at the desired level.*

If you find that you are doing everything you said you would, and doing them correctly, but the quality is not what was agreed to, then you will need to develop a quality improvement plan to bring quality to the desired level, or else redefine the level of quality that is acceptable. It may be that your company has overstated the level of quality that they are willing to pay for. Perhaps the cost of labor skilled enough to produce a high-quality finish on a piece of furniture cannot be justified based on the projected profit. In either case, a change control system should be in place to allow you to make these corrections.

QUALITY CONTROL

Quality control is the internal mechanism of monitoring the process to ensure that it remains under control and can reliably produce the desired level of quality.

It involves measuring and monitoring project and product variables to the quality standards that were agreed to and determining if they are within the acceptable range.

This exercise requires that you have a basic knowledge of statistical process control related to sampling techniques and probability distributions, although the sampling and control techniques are usually set up by your quality control group or outside consultants.

You need to know some statistics!

This assures that the results can be considered valid and defensible. I will cover these basic ideas shortly.

Note the difference

Some of the concepts involved in quality control include:

▶ *Prevention.* This means using the techniques to keep the process in control so that errors or defects *do not occur.*

▶ *Inspection.* This means using sampling and measuring methods to ensure that a defective finished product *does not reach the customer.*

▶ *Attribute sampling.* This is a binary test; either the product complies or it does not. It is also known as a "GO-NO GO" test. For example a part may be acceptable if it is between 10mm and 11mm. The actual measurement does not matter; just that it is in the range. 10.5 mm would be acceptable, but 11.1 mm would not.

▶ *Variable sampling.* This is where a test is done and the results are compared to a continuous scale; for instance, comparing the object's color to a predetermined chart.

▶ *Cause.* This is usually broken down into two categories:

- *Special or specific causes.* A clearly identifiable event that has created a problem (may also be called an assignable cause). A power failure may prevent you from meeting a schedule update deadline, thereby impacting your compliance goal. These must be reacted to or explained.

- *Random causes.* These are normal variations in the process. As long as the process is within acceptable range, you should not react to these.

▶ *Ranges.* There are two types of ranges you should be familiar with:

> **Tolerance: what you sell by**
> **Control limits: what you**
> **manage the process by**

- *Tolerances.* These are essentially the acceptable limits of the product variable being measured. Think of them as specifications. You are guaranteeing that the variable will be within the +/– range specified. If you advertised that an activity would take 14 days +/– 2 days, and you did it in 13 days, you are within tolerance.

■ *Control limits.* These are the internal constraints that you place on the variable to ensure that you will catch any variation *before* it exceeds the tolerance.

There are a number of techniques that you can use to operate a quality control program. Some you should be familiar with for the exam are:

▶ *Inspection.* Also known as audits, reviews, and walkthroughs, inspections involve measuring and analyzing a component or segment of a project or product and determining if it meets specifications. Note that I did not say if it was within control limits. That is the function of a control chart. You should do inspections on both a periodic and random basis. Software subroutine tests and checking bolt torque are examples of inspection.

▶ *Pareto diagrams.* Pareto diagrams show all of the defects or problems ordered by frequency of occurrence (see Figure 8.1). This display is referred to as a *histogram* (a representation of a frequency distribution by means of rectangles whose widths represent class intervals and whose areas are proportional to the corresponding frequencies).

In this example, I have graphed six events of interest. Bear in mind that we generally think of

Remember the 80/20 rule

Pareto diagrams as displaying problems or defects, but they can be used to track positive events as well. Basically, they show

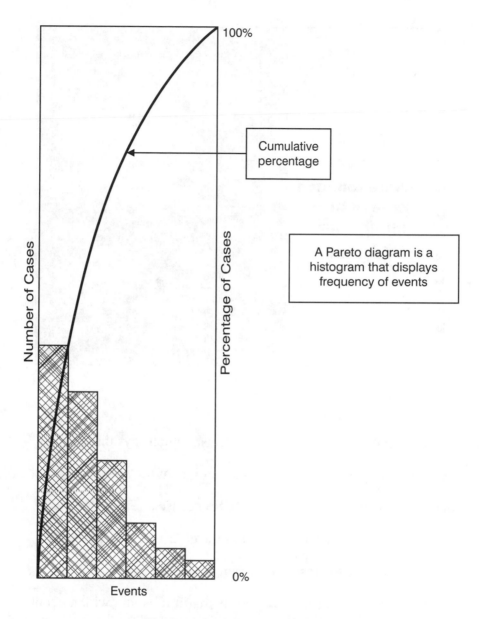

Figure 8.1   A Pareto Diagram

the events across the bottom and the frequency of occurrence on the vertical axis. The percentage and cumulative percentage are also useful. You may have heard of "Pareto's Law," named after

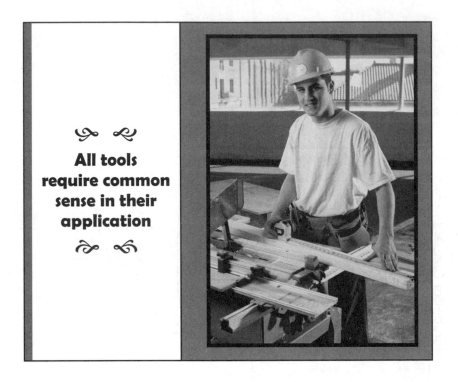

❧ ❧

All tools require common sense in their application

❧ ❧

the nineteenth-century Italian economist, which says that a small number of events (*the vital few*) cause most of the problems, while the majority of events (*the trivial many*) cause a relatively small number. This has become known as the 80/20 rule: 80 percent of the problems are the result of 20 percent of the causes.

The value of a Pareto diagram is that it tells you which event to work on first. In this case, event "A" has a significantly higher frequency of occurrence, so it should be addressed first. This assumes that the events are similar in impact—which may not be true. Assume for a minute that these events are airplane accidents, and "A" results in a broken light, but "F" results in the airplane falling out of the sky! Which should you work on first? Fortunately, most events that you will track are not so potentially catastrophic. Like any tool, Pareto diagrams provide information, not solutions.

▶ *Control charts.* These are charts that track a variable over the course of time. They are used to record the value of a variable or event at a fixed frequency to monitor how much it is changing (see Figure 8.2). The data can be entered manually or automatically. There is much to be said for having the operator physically take the measurement, enter the data point, and draw the line. Something about being "in the process" makes the operator more aware of the direction that the results are taking. Simply looking at a computer screen may not have the same effect.

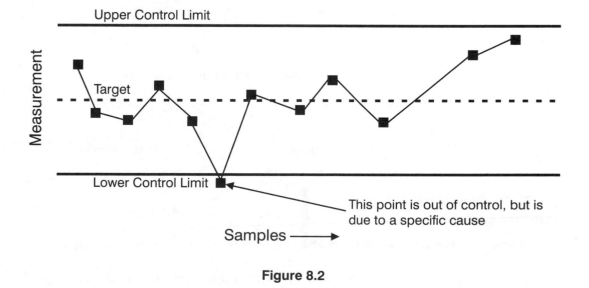

Figure 8.2

There are a number of definitions you should know in order to understand control charts:

Here are the statistics I told you about

- *Standard deviation (SIGMA).* The standard deviation is a statistical measure of how closely to the mean (average) a set of data points is grouped. It is used to analyze the variability of a process. It is also used to establish the control limits within

This is not as difficult as it may seem

which the process should operate. Using the concept of a normal distribution, you can decide just how tight to make your quality standards. For example, consider the following:

+/– 1 standard deviation = 68.26% of the population

+/– 2 standard deviations = 95.46% of the population

+/– 3 standard deviations = 99.73% of the population

+/– 6 standard deviations = 99.99% of the population

This means that if you set your limits at 1 standard deviation,

Higher sigma numbers means tighter control

less than 70 percent of the samples you measure will fall within the acceptable range. At 2 standard deviations, over 95 percent will be acceptable. Three sigma and six sigma represent much tighter limits, although the difference between the two is minor. Remember that higher standard deviations mean tighter control.

■ *Control limits.* There are two control limits on a control chart. The upper control limit shows the highest, and the lower control limit shows the lowest, measurements allowable to still have the process in control. These limits are typically set at either three standard deviations or six standard deviations, depending on your organization's quality expectations. Only after repeated measurements of the process, and the necessary statistical analysis, can control limits be set. Two important concepts about control limits bear exploring:

✓ If the process is operating within the control limits that have been established,

> **A process that is in control should not be adjusted!**

it is in control and should not be adjusted. If you want to reduce the variability, you can *modify* the process to make it more robust and less variable.

✓ You cannot set control limits more restraining than the process is capable of performing. This is why they must be set after a detailed statistical analysis. Setting them tighter than the process can provide is inviting failure.

≫ ≪

**Setting tight
limits cannot
make a weak
process strong**

≫ ≪

For example, suppose you are assigned the task of
maintaining the temperature of a stream of water by using two
valves; one controlling the hot water, and the other controlling
the cold, much like your morning shower. In a modern home,
with adequate water pressure, this is pretty easy. However, in an
old apartment building with a single hot-water supply, it can be
pretty tricky. Your control limits can only be as tight as your
process variables are robust.

■ *Specifications.* These are upper and/or lower limits that represent
the customer's expectations and what you have agreed to
provide. They are above and/or below the control limits. A

process that cannot operate within specifications is defective and
must be modified.

- *Rule of seven.* The rule of seven states that if seven
  consecutive data points are clustered above or below the
  target, or if seven consecutive data points move up or down
  together, the process is out of control *even if all seven are
  within the control limits*. A process that is in control will
  show random measurements.

▶ *Statistical sampling.* At the heart of any control system is the concept of statistical sampling. The concept has been well researched
and documented. It basically in-
volves checking a portion of the

> **Statistical sampling is a proven concept that saves time and money**

production (sample) and extrap-
olating the information to de-
velop a profile of the entire lot (population). This is done for a
variety of reasons:

- Time: to check every bottle of shampoo coming off of an
  assembly line would be a daunting task.
- Cost: the staff required to check 100 percent of the production
  would be cost prohibitive.
- Practicality: to open every can of beer on a production line to
  check the alcohol content would destroy the entire lot!

CONCLUSION

While the topic of quality is most often thought of in terms of manufacturing or production, there are many project areas where quality management can play a vital role. Areas such as cost and schedule lend themselves to quality management given the right metrics.

The responsibility for producing a quality project or product lies with all involved. However, certain individuals may assume a lead role. Overall quality responsibility lies with management, either operating or the project manager. However, ultimate responsibility lies with the individuals and their commitment to quality.

AREAS OF EMPHASIS IN THIS CHAPTER

The following are some of the key elements covered in this chapter and in the PMBOK:

- ▶ The three phases of quality management
  - ▪ Quality planning: deciding on the level of quality
  - ▪ Quality assurance: ensuring the systems are in place to monitor quality
  - ▪ Quality control: using the tools to actually monitor quality
- ▶ International Organization for Standardization (ISO)
- ▶ Gold plating (PMI loves this term)
- ▶ Project quality versus product quality

- ▶ Quality versus grade

  - ▪ Quality means it meets the standards set for the item

  - ▪ Grade means it satisfies the level of sophistication required

- ▶ Prevention versus inspection

  - ▪ Prevention: keeping the defect from occurring

  - ▪ Inspection: keeping the defect from reaching the customer

- ▶ Sampling

  - ▪ Attribute

  - ▪ Variable

- ▶ Causes

  - ▪ Specific

  - ▪ Random

- ▶ Ranges

  - ▪ Tolerance

  - ▪ Control limits

- ▶ Pareto diagrams

  - ▪ 80 / 20 rule

  - ▪ Event histogram

- ▶ Control charts

  - ▪ Standard deviation

  - ▪ Control limits

    - ✓ Upper and lower

    - ✓ Do not adjust the process if it is within control limits

✓ Control limits must be statistically determined and cannot be

arbitrary

✓ Rule of seven: an indication that the process is out of control

▶ Statistical sampling

■ Time

■ Cost

■ Practicality

SAMPLE QUESTIONS: CHAPTER 8—SELECT THE *BEST* ANSWER

1. A Pareto diagram is a method of:

    A. Quality assessment

    B. Quality assurance

    C. Quality planning

    D. Quality control

2. ISO stands for:

    A. International Organization for Standardization

    B. International Organization for Specifications

    C. International Operation for Specifications

    D. None of the above

3. Ishikawa diagrams can be used for:

    A. Quality control

    B. Quality assessment

    C. Quality planning

    D. Quality assurance

4. The upper control limit defines:

    A. The highest specification limit that the customer wants

    B. The highest level that the process should operate within

    C. The standard deviation of the process

    D. The variance of the process

5. What is the standard deviation?

    A. A measure of central tendency

    B. A measure of dispersion

    C. The same as the control limit

    D. A measure of quality

6. The team determines that the product would benefit from additions that are beyond the agreed-to specifications. This is an example of:

    A. Scope change

    B. Change order

    C. Gold plating

    D. Quality assessment

7. Which of the following statements is true?

    A. Grade means that the product is appropriately designed for the intended end use

    B. Grade means that the product is designed to the highest standards

    C. Grade is the same as quality

    D. Quality means that the product is appropriately designed for its intended use

8. Which of the following represents 99.73 percent of the population?

    A. 2 sigmas from the mean

B. 3 standard deviations from the median

C. 3 sigmas from the mean

D. 2 standard deviations from the mode

9. If there are seven data points either above or below the mean, but still within the control limits, what should you do?

   A. Reject the product

   B. Reinspect the product

   C. Find the cause because this means that the process is out of control

   D. Ignore it and continue to measure the process

10. Quality is:

    A. Conformance to specifications

    B. Conformance to grade

    C. Conformance to the customer's desires

    D. Conformance to the project team's requirements

11. Prevention means:

    A. Keeping the defect from getting to the customer

    B. Keeping the defect from happening

    C. Keeping the process always on target, or mean

    D. Avoiding scope changes

12. Determining if a product conforms to a specification or does not (GO NO-GO) is an example of:

    A. Variable sampling

    B. Quality assurance

    C. Grade conformance

    D. Attribute sampling

13. Who has primary responsibility for quality in a project?

    A. The engineering staff

    B. The individual employees

    C. The customer

    D. The project manager

14. What is a quality audit?

    A. A structured procedure to ensure that the methods and standards agreed to are being followed

    B. A checklist for performing quality tests

    C. The result of inspections

    D. The result of prevention

15. Pareto's Law postulates that:

    A. 80 percent of the events create 80 percent of the problems

    B. 20 percent of the events create 20 percent of the problems

C. 20 percent of the events create 80 percent of the problems

D. Things that can go wrong will go wrong

16. Cause-and-effect diagrams (Ishikawa or fishbone diagrams) can be used to:

A. Improve thinking by forcing the team to look into the underlying reasons for events

B. Find blame for mistakes

C. Run the quality control program

D. Project the outcome of events into the future

17. If the process is operating randomly within the agreed-to control limits, the process can be considered:

A. Out of control because of the random variation

B. In control because of the random variation

C. In need of adjustment

D. In need of improvement

18. "Any diagram that shows how the various elements of a system relate" is the PMBOK definition of:

A. Benchmarking

B. Quality control

C. Quality policy

D. Flowchart

19. What is statistical sampling?

   A. Inspecting random units and using the information to deter-mine the characteristics of the population

   B. Inspecting every unit to determine specifications

   C. Inspecting a small number of units and using the information to understand the entire production

   D. Both A and C

20. Which of these statements about tolerance and control limits is true?

   A. Tolerance means that the measurement falls within the agreed-upon process limits

   B. Control limits mean that the measurement falls within the agreed-upon process limits

   C. Tolerance is the same as control limits

   D. Control limits are the same as specifications

Chapter 9

Human Resource Management

Human resource management questions are generally pretty easy, especially if you have had any formal education or coursework in the subject. Many questions will come from "General Knowledge" and "General Management Skills" covered in Chapter 2; however, you should understand the framework from the PMBOK. Also, there have been questions about motivational theories—these are not covered by PMI, so I will cover those as well.

I want you to consider the topic of human resources management from a project perspective as opposed to that of a continuing operation. This is for a number of reasons:

▶ Among those asked to participate, the temporary nature of a project may cause some concern regarding future employment and the reward system. In a matrix organization people often report to two different supervisors, and the supervisor doing the performance evaluation may not be in a position to observe the people doing the work.

Consider the topic of human resource management from a project perspective

▶ Contract personnel may be obtained to fill in skills that the team needs. This may cause resentment among the permanent staff.

▶ Throughout the project, the landscape will keep changing. The team developed for the detailed engineering may be all wrong for the field construction phase, even though there is a tendency to use them for "continuity." Also, the reporting structure will likely change throughout the phases of the project

The topic of human resource management is divided into three topics:

▶ *Organizational planning:* Designing the organization

▶ *Staff acquisition:* Arranging for the people to fill the roles identified during planning

► *Team development:* Getting the team members to work together to meet the project goals

ORGANIZATIONAL PLANNING

This involves identifying, documenting, and assigning roles and responsibilities and reporting relationships. This is often done in conjunction with the communications plan since the two are so closely linked.

Note that assigning does not necessarily mean putting individual names in the organizational chart. This phase is more about assigning responsibilities to *organizations*, such as purchasing, engineering, legal, and so on.

The PMBOK suggests that there are several inputs to the process of organization planning, including:

► *Organizational interfaces:* How are the various organizations (marketing, purchasing, accounting, manufacturing) going to handle interdepartmental relationships? In the changing nature of projects, the "driving organization" may well change throughout the project.

► *Technical interfaces:* This is the relationship between units within a department, such as accounts payable and accounts receivable, or between disciplines with engineering.

► *Interpersonal interfaces:* Relationships among the people on the project. Sometimes this can be informal, but on large or complex

෭ ෨

**You have
to know what
skills you
need to do the
project**

෪ ෫

projects, control over who can deal with whom is needed to avoid
confusion and conflict.

▶ *Staffing requirements:* You have to know what skills are needed to
do the project.

▶ *Constraints:* These are very real limits on your ability to staff the
project properly. If you have to hire a consultant because the organization lacks certain skills, you had better hope that this was included when the budget was established. You may also have to use
union labor due to an existing collective bargaining agreement.
This may limit you in terms of skills and/or availability.

The project organization design will depend a great deal on how the parent organization is organized and its existing personnel policies. For instance, in a matrix or-

ganization, responsibility for performance review and compensation can remain with the administrative manager or be delegated to the operational manager. Perhaps a peer-review system would be used to ensure that the individual is fairly appraised. (Chapter 2 goes into detail about organizational structures, so I am not going to repeat it here.)

The results of organization planning include several very important documents:

▶ *Roles and responsibility assignment.* This critical document describes *who does what* (roles) and *who gets to decide what* (responsibilities). This must be worked very closely with the scope, WBS, and communications plan to ensure that all aspects of the project have been assigned to someone. PMI uses the term Responsibility Assignment Matrix (RAM) to describe a document that identifies by name who is responsible for each aspect of the project, and what their particular responsibility, such as accountable, supporting, approve, etc., is. *Note that PMI is sending a mixed message in this section, as some of the "responsibilities" on the "RAM" on page 111 of the PMBOK are actually "roles."*

▶ *Organization chart.* This is a document that displays graphically who reports to whom.

▶ *Staffing management plan.* This often-forgotten document details when people are going to join the project and when they are scheduled to be released back to their parent organization, so they will not feel like they are being orphaned or forgotten. Another element of a staffing management plan has to do with working and living conditions when the staff is located away from home base. As we will see later, it is difficult to concentrate on work when you have no place to live! Parts of the staffing management plan are often displayed as a histogram, a bar chart showing different classes of staff hours across time.

STAFF ACQUISITION

Once the plan is in place, you need to actually recruit and/or assign individuals to the positions identified in the organizational chart. Some considerations for staffing acquisition are:

- ▶ Are there people with relevant experience?
- ▶ Does the individual being considered want to do the work?
- ▶ Does the individual display an ability to work with a team? Some people can do the work but have difficulty working with others.
- ▶ Do you have people available with the right competency? Bear in mind that experience and competence are two different things.
- ▶ Are there policies governing staff selection regarding seniority, ethnicity, sex, age, or other characteristics, such as union status?
- ▶ What are the policies and procedures if you have to go outside the organization?
- ▶ Do you have to personally negotiate with functional managers to obtain people, or is someone else in that role?

▶ Does any of the staff, such as construction personnel or a computer system hardware manager, come pre-assigned with procurement contracts?

Once you have answered these questions, you will begin collecting your staff. You need to complete the organizational chart, staff directory, communications plan, and the organizational breakdown structure (OBS) if one is used. An OBS is a special form of the WBS in which the names of the people responsible for a given task are entered.

TEAM DEVELOPMENT

Team development is critical if the team is to function properly. It is so critical that most organizations ignore it altogether! Some of the activities associated with team development are:

▶ *Team building.* This involves ensuring that the team understands the background, vision, and goals of the project, as well as the steps in the mission to accomplish these goals—and has the chance to give input into the project. This is also referred to as *alignment.* Unfortunately, team building is usually done in a superficial manner and is therefore ineffective. This ineffectiveness further erodes the organization's view of team building. A few of the mistakes that people make include:

■ Not involving everyone. In a construction project, it is not unusual for the owner and engineer to work together for months or years before the contractor is hired. Even if the owner and engineer had a successful team development exercise, it is often not repeated when the contractor joins the team. The contractor is going to spend most of the budget. Would it not seem that they should be integrated into the team?

- Going out to dinner, having a speech about how great we are and going home is *not* team building. However, it is one of the most common ways that organizations claim they are doing it!

- Not following through. Team building is a *continuous process.*

- Lack of sincerity and commitment by senior management.

- Not using the team building exercise(s) to develop tools for handling conflict or other disruptions to the project.

▶ *General management skills.* Chapter 2 covers general management skills. One that is not fully covered, however, is conflict management. Conflicts are a way of life in projects, and it is foolhardy to assume that they will go away if ignored. Conflicts almost always arise from something other than personality conflicts, although I think if you did a survey, you would get a different answer. Conflicts usually involve people getting mixed information about such things as schedule, priorities, procedures, and technical issues. As such, the source of the conflict needs to be addressed and eliminated.

There are several recognized conflict resolution techniques:

- *Problem solving.* Confronting and solving the real problem, not just the symptom

- *Compromising.* Getting agreement on a middle ground (this almost always just postpones the problem)

- *Withdrawing.* Avoiding solving the problem

- *Smoothing.* Emphasizing what is going well rather than focusing on the problem

- *Forcing.* Having your way at the expense of others

    PMI suggests that problem solving is the best method, and forcing is the worst!

▶ *Reward and recognition systems.* These are systems that tie results to rewards. About the only thing to remember here is that if you are going to hold someone accountable for achieving a goal, you must give them the means and authority to accomplish the goal.

▶ *Training.* You are responsible for seeing that your team members are trained to handle the tasks that are assigned. They are responsible for letting you know if they need training.

▶ *Facilities.* I touched on this earlier. The facilities that are provided to the team represent a very important aspect of the project. I once worked for a company that did projects away from the office. They would relocate the staff so that they would all be together. The home office purchasing manager was responsible for housing and would generally offer a choice of hotel or apartment. The problem was that he would deal only with the absolute lowest-quality buildings with the most spartan of furnishings, and it affected morale. Only after he was assigned to a remote project did this change! Other considerations—such as noisy offices, insufficient supplies or support—can all lead to problems on the project.

MOTIVATING WORKERS AND THE SOURCES OF POWER

Throughout the past 100 years, the thinking on what motivates people has changed dramatically. Since your job is to motivate people, I want to provide a summary of some relevant theories. This material has appeared on the exam under the umbrella of general knowledge. It is not covered in the PMBOK.

Frederick Taylor: Scientific Management

Frederick Taylor was an engineer that published his work in 1911. He was viewed as an early "Efficiency Expert." He espoused that work should be broken down into the smallest possible units, and that management should design the activities needed to perform the work. Labor's job was to follow these directions. This sort of robotic approach apparently seemed appropriate for the fledgling "assembly-line method." I am afraid there are some Taylor followers out there even now!

Abraham Maslow: Hierarchy of Needs

Maslow published his work in the late 1960s. He envisioned a pyramid-shaped presentation of needs, and held that you could not achieve higher-level needs until all of the ones below had been satisfied. (This is why, for example, poor living conditions on a project can impact performance.)

Douglas McGregor: The Human Side of Enterprise

Also published in the 1960s, McGregor held that assumptions about workers could be divided into two groups, Theory X and Theory Y:

Theory X:

People need to be watched at all times. They must be told what to do and how to do it, as they are incapable of planning their own work and will avoid work if at all possible.

Theory Y:

People are willing and capable of managing their own work if given the means and methods to do so.

Frederick Herzberg: Two-Factor Hygiene and Motivation Theory

Herzberg published his work in 1959. It holds that there are two distinct classes of motivators that influence people:

▶ Hygiene factors: These are things such as:

- Salary

- Working conditions

- Policies

- Status

- Security

The common link with these is that the *lack* of them can lead to a lowering of motivation, but improving them may only motivate people for a short time. This is the problem with trying to motivate people with money—it only provides a short-term impact.

▶ Motivating factors: These are things that relate to what people actually *do* on the job. They are such things as:

- Achievement

- Recognition

- Responsibility

- Growth

- Interest in the work

French and Raven: The Bases of Social Power

In 1968, John French and Bertram Raven published a work that examined the sources of power in social situations. You need to understand this, because you must get things done to finish the project but you may not actually have the power to do it! Therefore, you need to know how people respond within a social situation.

French and Raven identified five bases of power:

▶ *Reward.* This is the ability to offer rewards or incentives to get people to do what is desired. Performance appraisal systems are an example of such rewards, as are commission and incentive programs for salesmen.

▶ *Coercive.* The boss has the power to make you do what he wants—assuming you intend to stay employed!

▶ *Legitimate.* The organization has assigned you as the project manager and formally given you the authority over the project staff.

▶ *Referent.* This is based on admiration and respect. People exhibit referent power when others seek their approval, although this approval is not required for the decision in question.

▶ *Expert.* A person to whom others look as a source of knowledge has expert power. Technically trained people who are not in charge can nonetheless exhibit expert power.

▶ *Information.* Later, French and Raven added a sixth basis concerning the rapidly expanding information age. A database manager, for example, has tremendous influence and power in the organization, especially if he or she controls the e-mail system!

CONCLUSION

Even though the exam places little emphasis on human resources, I think that it is important for you to study this chapter, mainly because many project managers have been put into their positions with little or no training in the subject of managing people. It is all too common for highly skilled technical people to be promoted into management because it is assumed that they will do that job as well as they did their technical work. This is called the "halo effect." Imagine if you will a crew of carpenters in need of a foreman. It is likely that the best carpenter will be promoted because of the halo effect. What you have now is an inexperienced foreman running a crew that just lost its best carpenter!

You owe it to yourself—but more especially, to your future staff—to understand how to manage people.

AREAS OF INTEREST IN THIS CHAPTER

The following are some of the key elements covered in this chapter and in the PMBOK:

- ▶ Phases of human resource management
  - Organizational planning
  - Staff acquisition
  - Team development
- ▶ General management skills

▶ The influence of the temporary nature of the project versus the permanent nature of continuing operations

▶ Project interfaces

  ■ Organizational

  ■ Technical

  ■ Interpersonal

▶ Constraints

▶ Roles and responsibilities

  ■ Responsibility Assignment Matrix (RAM)

▶ Staffing management plan

▶ Organizational breakdown structure

▶ Resource histogram

▶ Staffing pool description

  ■ Experience

  ■ Interest

  ■ Compatibility

  ■ Availability

  ■ Competence

▶ Team development

  ■ Team building

  ■ Rewards and recognition

  ■ Facilities

▶ Motivation and power

- Taylor's Scientific Management

- Maslow's Hierarchy of Needs

- McGregor's Theory X - Theory Y

- Herzberg's Two-Factor Hygiene and Motivators

- French and Raven's Bases of Social Power

SAMPLE QUESTIONS: CHAPTER 9—SELECT THE *BEST* ANSWER

1. Which is the most effective way to deal with conflict?

    A. Ignore it

    B. Smooth things out

    C. Confront the problem

    D. Coercing

2. The top three sources of conflict are:

    A. Personality, schedule, and cost

    B. Procedures, personality, and technical opinions

    C. Schedule, project priorities, and resources

    D. Project priorities, cost, and personality

3. Frederick Taylor believed:

    A. Workers were lazy and did not want to work

    B. Work should be broken down into the smallest manageable pieces, and procedures written to perform it

    C. That there are a variety of sources of power

    D. Hygiene factors are strong motivators

4. According to the PMBOK, what are the three primary interfaces that occur during organizational planning?

    A. Organizational, technical, and interpersonal

    B. Technical, managerial, and organizational

    C. Organizational, structural, and interpersonal

    D. Technical, interpersonal, and procedural

5. What are constraints?

    A. Restrictions placed on you by management

    B. Restrictions placed on you by other stakeholders

    C. Restrictions placed on you by law and government policies

    D. All of the above are constraints

6. What did Maslow conclude in his study of motivation?

    A. People are motivated by money

    B. People are inherently trustworthy and want to do a good job

    C. You cannot concentrate on higher-level needs until you have
        satisfied lower-level needs

    D. Information control is a source of power

7. Assuming that a person can do other things well because he or
    she is currently exhibiting excellent performance is an example of:

    A. The halo effect

    B. The competency paradox

    C. The Doppler effect

    D. The Hawthorne effect

8. A document that details who has responsibility for various aspects
    of a project is called:

    A. An organization chart

    B. A staffing plan

    C. A responsibility assignment matrix

    D. A WBS

9.   Which of the following would be a highly effective method of team development?

  A.   Dinner and speeches

  B.   An alignment session

  C.   A series of meetings between the project manager and the individual staff members

  D.   A teleconference with senior management

10.   Which of the following statements is most pertinent with regard to facilities?

  A.   Fancy offices are a sign of prestige

  B.   Elaborate facilities are the only way to get staff to go to remote locations

  C.   Worrying about inadequate facilities distracts the team from concentrating on good performance

  D.   Really dedicated staff won't care about facilities, just the project

11.   Wanting approval from someone well respected in the organization is an example of which type of power?

  A.   Expert

  B.   Referent

  C.   Legitimate

  D.   Reward

12. What is a resource histogram?

    A. An organization chart

    B. The same thing as an OBS

    C. A chart showing responsibility

    D. A bar graph showing the amounts of resources needed by
       time period

13. Which of the following types of power is not bestowed upon an in-
    dividual by the organization?

    A. Coercive and legitimate

    B. Referent and reward

    C. Expert and referent

    D. Legitimate and referent

14. Which of the following statements represents how the PMBOK dif-
    ferentiates between *roles* and *responsibilities*?

    A. Roles are what people do, while responsibilities indicate their
       decision-making authority

    B. Roles represent decision-making authority, while responsibili-
       ties are what people do

    C. Roles represent reporting relationships, while responsibilities
       represent what people do

    D. Responsibilities and roles are interchangeable

15. That you should know certain skills, such as communicating, coaching, and negotiating is referred to as

    A. Legitimate power

    B. Project management skills

    C. General management skills

    D. Organizational skills

Chapter 10

Communications Management

According to the PMBOK, "project communications management includes the processes required to ensure timely and appropriate generation, collection, dissemination, storage, and ultimate disposition of project information" (PMBOK 2000, p. 117). Communications management has to do with determining who needs information, when they need it, and how will it be transmitted. It *does not* include the act of communicating itself, although this is certainly an important area with which every project manager should be familiar. The art of communication is not specific to project management. It deals with such things as how to write effectively, whether to communicate verbally or in writing, sender-receiver models such as barriers to communication, and so on.

Every project plan should contain a communications plan that addresses these questions. The importance of such a plan cannot be overstated. Projects live or die by the flow of information, and many problems occur simply because various stakeholders are not kept informed. I was told by John Cashman, who flew the first

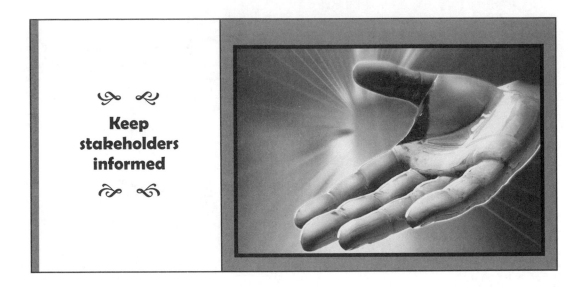

Keep stakeholders informed

777 airplane, that the team developed a communications plan early in the program, and that the result was people saying, "Oh, that's why they're doing that. I wondered about that." Furthermore, they referred to the big jet as *our* airplane. Being kept constantly informed gave them a sense of belonging to the entire team and a sense of ownership.

COMMUNICATIONS MANAGEMENT PROCESSES

There are four primary processes listed in the PMBOK for communications management:

1. *Communications planning.* Determining the information needs of all stakeholders—who needs what information, how frequently they need it, and how will it be given to them.

2. *Information distribution.* The process of making needed information available to those who need it in a timely manner.

3. *Performance reporting.* Collecting and distributing information on progress. This includes measuring progress, reporting status, and forecasting future results.

4. *Administrative closure.* This includes gathering information and generating and disseminating information about a phase or final project closeout.

Communications Planning

Not all stakeholders to a project have the same needs for information. The first step in communication planning is to identify all stakeholders and then survey them to determine their information needs. This will be discussed below. Communications planning

> **Stakeholder: anyone who has a vested interest in a project, including customers, contributors, suppliers, senior managers, the project sponsor, and all project team members.**

is often tied to organizational planning, since the organization structure of the project will affect how information is disseminated. In addition, while it is not specifically covered by the PMBOK, as the size of a project team grows so does the overhead cost of communication. This overhead can, in fact, be very substantial. The project manager may struggle to keep everyone informed of what is going on. This is because the number of channels of communications is given by the following equation:

$$C = N (N-1)/2$$

where C is the number of channels of communication, and N is the number of individuals that are involved in the communication. This has been the subject of questions on the exam, so lets do an example.

A question may ask: *If there are four people on the team, and three more join, how many more channels of communication are added?*

Channels with 4 members = $4 (4-1)/2 = 6$

Channels with 7 members = $7 (7-1)/2 = 21$

So, adding three people increased the number of channels by 15! (Note that the answer is not 6 or 21.)

This simple example demonstrates how critical it is to develop a communications plan.

Inputs to Communications Planning

Communications Requirements   There is often a temptation to communicate everything to everyone—or nothing to anyone—but this can quickly become a significant burden. As was shown above, as the number of participants in a project grows so does the number of channels over which information flows. If the amount of information also increases, it can overwhelm the communications network. People then begin to suffer from information overload. It is therefore important that only information necessary for the correct functioning of the project be disseminated, and only to those stakeholders who actually need it. Another way to think of this is that the only information that should be communicated is that which contributes to success or could lead to failure if not communicated.

To determine communications requirements, you should consider the following:

- ▶ The project organization and stakeholder responsibilities
- ▶ Disciplines, departments, and specialties involved in the project
- ▶ The number of individuals involved at a project and at what locations
- ▶ External parties that want information, such as the media

Communications Technology   The methods used to convey information among all project stakeholders can vary considerably, from brief face-to-face encounters in hallways to formal meetings, e-mail, internet-accessible databases, and video conferencing. Some factors that may affect the communications plan include:

- ▶ Immediacy needs of stakeholders. That is, do some individuals need almost real-time information about the project, or can they use simple, periodic reports?
- ▶ Availability of technology. Are the systems already in place, or would they have to be developed?
- ▶ Skills of project team members. Will team members already have the skills necessary to operate required technology, or must training be provided?

The methods used to convey information among all project stakeholders can vary considerably

▶ Project duration. Will technology change over the life of the project? If so, must these changes be incorporated into the project?

Constraints   Constraints are factors that will limit a project team's options for communication. For example, projects in which work is contracted out will require different communications than those in which all work is done internally.

Assumptions   We discussed assumptions in Chapter 4, and these will not be revisited other than to say that all projects involve assumptions that must be clarified to avoid later problems.

Tools and Techniques for Communications Planning

Stakeholder Analysis   It is important to understand the information needs of all stakeholders, and to ensure that they receive that information in a timely manner, using the appropriate technology. Discussion of stakeholders is contained in Chapter 2.

Outputs from Communications Planning

Communications Management Plan   Obviously, the purpose of communications management planning is to produce documents that prescribe how communications in the project are to be handled. This document will be the communications management plan. The plan should specify the following:

**Constraints
are factors that
will limit a
project team's
options for
communication**

▶ How will information be collected and filed, and in what format? What procedure will be used to update documents and ensure that everyone has the latest revision? This is very important, as failure to control revisions can lead to some members of the project team working with obsolete schedules. Usually a revision number is attached to a document, together with a date, so that you can quickly determine if the document is the most recent version (as long as the document control index is kept current).

▶ What information should be collected? In what format will it be distributed? What level of detail will be provided? Are specific terms to be used in specific ways? If so, these should be identified.

▶ Who should receive what information? How will it be distributed? Not all stakeholders need all information. There must be a distribution matrix that specifies this. Examples of how information is distributed include written reports, meetings, and face-to-face verbal communication. In the event of widely dispersed teams, this may be supplemented by e-mail, teleconferencing, and so on. Documents may also be distributed electronically, using either PDF files or native files (doc, xls, msp, etc.).

▶ A production and distribution schedule. How often will each kind of information be collected and distributed? In some projects, project status data is collected and distributed weekly. In others, the schedule may be monthly.

▶ Is there any method of accessing information in between scheduled distributions?

▶ A procedure for revising the communications plan as the need arises. For example, when stakeholders change the distribution list must change.

The communications plan may be formal or informal, highly structured or not, as the needs of the project dictate.

Information Distribution

Perhaps it is obvious, but information has no value unless it reaches the appropriate individuals involved in the project. Furthermore, that information must be in the proper format and must be timely. Often, because of flaws in the communications system, information reaches a person too late for them to act on it in the required manner. Also, even though the PMBOK does not discuss it, people in today's world tend to suffer from information overload, which can result in project communications being overlooked or ignored by the intended recipient. Information distribution involves implementing the communications plan and also responding to unplanned requests for information.

Again, the PMBOK does not discuss distributing anything but information about work results. Nevertheless, stakeholders are concerned about events that may affect the work, organizational changes, and other events that could impact the project either positively or negatively.

Tools and Techniques for Information Distribution

Communications Skills   Communication is a two-way street. In involves not only the dissemination of information but the receiving of it as well. The PMBOK says that the sender is responsible for ensuring that information is clear, unambiguous, and complete, and that the receiver is responsible for making sure that information is received in its entirety and is understood correctly. I disagree with this, but if it is asked on the exam, give the PMBOK answer.

Here is the problem. The receiver cannot be held responsible for communication. Only the sender has that responsibility, and I must ensure that the intended message was received *and* understood. An example of this is seen in air traffic control. I was flying into Chicago's O'Hare airport on a United flight, and at the time they had an audio channel on which you could listen to air traffic. The controller told a pilot to descend to a certain altitude and fly 300 knots exactly. The pilot responded, "Roger. Descend to 6,000 and fly 300 or better." The controller replied, "Negative. 300 exactly!"

This is a system in which the receiver of the communication is expected to repeat back what he has heard, so that the sender can ensure that it was received correctly, and in this example the message was misunderstood. Had the controller not detected the misunderstanding, the plane would have been flying too fast, overtaking traffic ahead, and this could have been a disaster.

To make the point a little more strongly: how can the recipient of a communication know that she has misunderstood it? Clearly, she cannot. So the basic premise that we must remember as project managers is that responsibility for communication rests with the *communicator*, not with the recipient! That said, remember the PMBOK answer.

There are several dimensions to communications, and all of them can affect the ultimate outcome. These include:

▶ Written and oral, listening and speaking

▶ Internal (that is, within the project) and external—to the customer, the media, the public, and so on

▶ Formal (written reports, briefings, review meetings) and informal (casual memos, conversations in the hallway, and so on)

▶ Vertical (up and down the organizational hierarchy) and horizontal (with peers)

Information Retrieval Systems

One problem many of us have is finding information that we have filed away somewhere. In any case, information can be shared in projects through a number of methods, including manual and electronic filing systems, databases, project management software, and other information systems. Some of the information that project stakeholders may need includes technical drawings, design specifications, test plans, and personnel data. An information retrieval system should be designed so that people can access such information in a timely manner.

Marvin Patterson, in his book *Accelerating Innovation* (1992), has argued that a reference librarian can be a big help to a project team that relies on processing information to develop new products. Such an individual can provide that information in a just-in-time (JIT) manner, thus improving the performance of the project team.

Information Distribution Methods

The ways in which project information can be distributed are almost endless. Though not used (much) any more, smoke signals, carrier pigeons, and telegraphy are all possibilities! On a serious note, the conventional methods include formal meetings, the grapevine, document distribution in either electronic or hard-copy format, e-mail, the project intranet, and so on.

Outputs from Information Distribution

Project Records   These include memos, progress and status reports, purchase requisitions, correspondence, various documents describing the project, including revisions to the plan, and so on. These must be maintained in some organized fashion. A project notebook (which may actually occupy a number of binders for large projects) is one way to do this. The advantage of a notebook is that you have everything in one place, and it can serve as a convenient resource when doing lessons-learned reviews later on.

Project Reports   These are, of course, formal documents that detail project status and/or issues that need attention or have been dealt with.

Project Presentations   Project managers are often asked to make presentations to various stakeholders to keep them up to date on what is happening with the project. In fact, research has shown that projects are often judged negatively when stakeholders are not kept informed and when the project is not presented in a good light. It is therefore useful to "sell" your project—that is, present it in the best possible light to key stakeholders. The downside is that stakeholders can make heavy demands on project managers to keep them informed. I remember a project manager on a very large government project telling me that he spent about 60 percent of his time doing such presentations to members of Congress and several other stakeholders, so that if he had not had a project administrator managing the job day to day, it would have gotten into serious trouble.

Performance Reporting

Performance reporting involves the development and dissemination of documents and exhibits that show the status of the project at a given point in time. Typically, these are used to measure schedule and cost, but any number of other indicators, such as training, testing, or other project objectives, can be included. The process of performance reporting generally includes:

▶ *Status reporting:* Where does the project currently stand?

▶ *Progress reporting:* What has been accomplished since the last status report?

▶ *Forecasting:* What is expected to be accomplished in the next period?

Tools for performance reporting include:

▶ *Performance reviews.* These are typically meetings set up so that you can present the current status of the project. They can be formal or informal, and the depth of the content will depend on the audience. Senior management reviews can be more general than those for the engineering manager, although my experience is that senior managers cannot resist getting into the details—so be prepared.

▶ *Variance analysis.* This involves comparing the actual value of an item to what that value should be at this time. The list of items to be measured should have been developed during project plan development, which I covered in Chapter 4.

▶ *Trend analysis.* This is tracking performance over time to see if conditions are improving or deteriorating. An example might be the number of bricks laid in a shift. Trend analysis could point out problems with material supply or quality. Note that trend analysis is over time, while variance analysis focuses on a given point. (You can, of course, track the variance over time.)

▶ *Earned value analysis.* Earned value analysis (also called earned value management in the PMBOK) is a method of tracking schedule and cost variances together. I have covered earned value analysis in great detail in Chapter 7, and I will not go into it further here.

Performance reporting results in documents that will be distributed and archived for future use. Other outcomes might include:

▶ Change requests. It may be that a change in direction or emphasis might result from your review. Perhaps more staff will be needed. This will improve schedule at the expense of the budget. On the other hand, maybe things are going too well, and companion parts of the project will not be ready when you are finished.

▶ Budget adjustments.

▶ Scope additions or deletions.

▶ Firing the project manager!

Performance reporting should be done routinely and continue during administrative closure.

Administrative Closure

This is the process of documenting the results of your work to ensure that you have met all of the requirements and specifications. It should be done whenever a phase of the project is complete and at the end. This is valuable, since near the end of a project, team members are often re-assigned and are not available to participate. Some of the items to be considered during administrative closure include:

▶ Collecting and archiving all project documents, including final cost and schedule information.

▶ Updating records and specifications to reflect what actually happened on the project.

▶ Revising any employee databases to reflect current skills and understand future training needs.

▶ Developing the final project report that will assess just how the project went, and review the results of the project as it relates to the product that was made. Remember, well run projects can produce lousy products!

▶ Performing a lessons learned review that includes all stakeholders and team members

AREAS OF EMPHASIS IN THIS CHAPTER

The following are some of the key elements covered in this chapter and in the PMBOK:

▶ The phases of communication management

■ Communications planning

■ Information distribution

■ Performance reporting

- ■ Administrative closure

▶ Communication skills versus communication management

▶ The formula for the number of communication channels depending on how many people are involved $© = N\,(N-1)/2$

▶ Communications requirements and technology

▶ PMBOK's emphasis on the receiver being responsible for making sure she has gotten all of the information

▶ Performance Reporting

- ■ Status Reports

- ■ Progress reports

- ■ Forecasting

▶ Performance reporting tools

- ■ Performance reviews

- ■ Variance analysis

- ■ Trend analysis

- ■ Earned value analysis

▶ Administrative closure should be done after each phase

SAMPLE QUESTIONS: CHAPTER 10—SELECT THE *BEST* ANSWER

1. Who is responsible for ensuring that the communication actually delivered the information intended?

    A. The sender

    B. The receiver

    C. Both the sender and receiver

    D. The project communications coordinator

2   Which of the following is *not* a performance reporting method?

    A. Status reporting

    B. Forecasting

    C. Progress reporting

    D. Earned value analysis

3. The difference between communications skills and communications management is:

    A. Communications skills are techniques, while communications management is a plan

    B. Communications skills are a plan, while communications management is tool

    C. They are the same thing

    D. Communications skills are a subset of the communications plan

4. Complex information is best communicated:

   A. Informally and verbally

   B. Written and formally

   C. Verbally and formally

   D. Informally and written

5. What is earned value analysis?

   A. A form of trend analysis

   B. A form of status reporting

   C. A method of information distribution

   D. A technique for analyzing cost and schedule together

6. Making needed information available to project stakeholders in a timely manner is:

   A. Communications planning

   B. Administrative closure

   C. Information distribution

   D. Performance reporting

7. How many channels of communication are there when there are eight people involved?

   A. 12

   B. 8

   C. 56

   D. 28

8. Which of the following is not a result of information distribution?

    A. Variance analysis

    B. Project reports

    C. Project records

    D. Project presentations

9. Status reporting:

    A. Describes the progress made in the last reporting period

    B. Describes the condition of the project now

    C. Combines schedule and cost information in a single report

    D. Is an administrative closure technique

10. "Lessons learned" is a method used in which phase of communications management?

    A. Administrative closure

    B. Communications skills

    C. Performance reporting

    D. Negotiating methods

Chapter 11

Risk

INTRODUCTION

This chapter is intended to give you a full understanding of how risk can affect a project, and how to develop tools to identify, assess, and control risk. In order to better understand and apply the principles that will be discussed, I first want to provide an overview of risk in general and especially in a project environment.

First of all, I need to dispel the notion that all risk is bad. Risk is simply the eventuality that unknown things can happen. Risk is further divided into good risks, called opportunities, and bad risks, referred to as threats. For example, you cannot listen to any investing talk show, or read any articles on investing, without coming across the terms risk/reward or risk tolerance. In this context risk is bad; you could lose your money on a bad or "risky" investment. However, would the investment be any more risky if you had made money? Clearly the answer is no. The risk involved was that the outcome was not known at the time of the investment. There is a wide range of places to put your money, and some will be riskier than others. For example, U.S. Government treasuries are considered almost risk free. The chance

Risk:
an uncertain
event that may
occur

of default and the resulting loss of money are negligible. On the other hand, Third World municipal bonds are quite risky. The payoff is high *if* they deliver.

The old saying, "Nothing ventured, nothing gained," holds true in our investment example above and is true in projects as well. Starting a new project entails

Nothing ventured, nothing gained

dealing with many unknowns, some of which will have negative consequences. Others will have positive consequences, while the rest will be neutral—they are simply unknowns that have no impact.

The remainder of the chapter will concentrate on negative risks since these are the ones that you want to control. This is not to say that highly positive events are without consequence, but the organizational impact is generally less traumatic.

KEEPING THINGS IN PERSPECTIVE

However, before I get into the details of how the PMBOK discusses risk, I think it would be useful to review the method of thinking derived from the Allied Institute Automotive Group. This method, known as Failure Mode and Effects Analysis (FMEA), looks at three factors:

▶ The actual risk involved, and the probability that the risk will occur (O) (see Table 11.1)

▶ The severity of the outcome that would follow should the event happen (S) (see Table 11.2)

▶ Ease of detecting or recognizing that the risk is about to occur (D) (see Table 11.3)

Table 11.1

Probability of Failure	Possible Failure Rates	Rank
Very High: Failure is almost certain	≥ 1 in 2	10
	1 in 3	9
High: Repeated failures possible	1 in 8	8
	1 in 20	7
Moderate: Occasional failures	1 in 80	6
	1 in 400	5
	1 in 2,000	4
Low: Relatively few failures	1 in 15,000	3
	1 in 150,000	2
Remote: Failure is unlikely	≤ 1 in 1,500,000	1

Table 11.2

Effect	Criteria: Severity of Effect	Rank
Hazardous without Warning	Project severely impacted, possible cancellation with no warning	10
Hazardous with Warning	Project severely impacted, possible cancellation with warning	9
Very High	Major impact on project schedule, budget, or performance; may cause severe delays, overruns, or degradation of performance	8
High	Project schedule, budget, or performance impacted significantly; job can be completed, but customer will be very dissatisfied	7
Moderate	Project schedule, budget, or performance impacted some; customer will be dissatisfied	6
Low	Project schedule, budget, or performance impacted slightly; customer will be mildly dissatisfied	5
Very Low	Some impact to project; customer will be aware of impact	4
Minor	Small impact to project; average customer will be aware of impact	3
Very Minor	Impact so small that it would be noticed only by a very discrimination customer	2
None	No effect	1

Table 11.3

Detection	Rank
Absolute Uncertainty	10
Very Remote	9
Remote	8
Very Low	7
Low	6
Moderate	5
Moderately High	4
High	3
Very High	2
Almost Certain	1

Each of these should be assigned a value of 1 to 10, with 10 being the most severe.

Once these three factors have been assessed, the risk priority number (RPN) can be calculated. This RPN is an index of the overall project risk for any given factor. The value can be from 1 to 1,000, with 1,000 being a catastrophic failure that is certain to happen and cannot be detected! Wow, let's all hope we never see one of those.

> **RPN is a way to put risk in perspective**

The RPN will rank the risks that have been identified and allow you the opportunity to develop corrective plans for those with high a RPN. An element of judgment needs to be used here. It is often recommended that severity of the event should call for corrective actions, even when the probability and detection factors are low. In doing this exercise it is important for you to remain realistic. A tidal wave is unlikely and cannot be readily detected, but it would be a 10 in severity. You would be wise to not spend time developing a plan to deal with one.

It is also interesting to note that two risk situations can have the same RPN for very different reasons. To blindly prioritize risks by RPN could lead to errors in judgment, to say the least. Let's suppose the following circumstances, and compare the RPNs for each:

Risk: Having a supplier deliver equipment late

O	5
S	5
D	4
RPN	100

Risk: Being eaten by a shark

O	1
S	10
D	10
RPN	100

Unless your project is filming a documentary on the Great Barrier Reef, being eaten by a shark is not a viable threat. However, blindly following the RPN ranking and the severity admonition would result in your developing a plan for this risk. Obviously, I have selected an extreme example to demonstrate the point, but I did so to help you recognize the need to keep things in perspective.

With this thought pattern in mind as a way to view risk, let's begin the discussion of how the PMBOK handles risk analysis.

THE PMBOK ON RISK MANAGEMENT

The PMBOK recognizes nine different knowledge areas, which generally follow the familiar categories of scope, estimate, schedule, organization, and procurement that are commonly used in project work. The topic of risk management is at once a knowledge area and a concern in all of the process areas and other knowledge areas.

Because most project team members have no experience or formal training in risk management, I have organized this chapter to closely follow the outline of the PMBOK. There is a lot of unfamiliar material in the risk section of the PMBOK, so there is a good chance that there will be several questions on the test, and they may not be intuitive.

Risk Management Planning

In order to begin the risk analysis process, you first must develop a risk management plan. This, in general, is an outline of how you will control the risk process. The risk management plan must be developed early and revisited throughout the various phases of the project. A major shortcoming of most risk management exercises is that the plan is developed too late, and never reviewed again.

Major topics included as inputs to the risk management plan include:

▶ *Project charter.* As covered in scope development, the project charter is the document that defines the business needs of the project and the description of the product to be produced. It serves as authorization for the project to go forward. It can be in the form of a contract, appropriation, or other organization-specific document.

▶ *Risk management policies.* If your organization has a defined policy regarding risk, you should include it in the plan. If a formal policy does not exist, some thought should be given to developing an *ad hoc* version for the project. This will serve as a guide for future assessment and can be a model for a formal set of policies.

▶ *Defined roles and responsibilities.* You should establish authority for decisions, and this should be documented and included in the plan. In this way, all team members will be able to identify the lead decision maker on the various steps in the analysis. For example, if the procurement department is solely responsible for contract paperwork, then they should take the lead in any exercise involving their department's risk policies. These policies should be open for review by the rest of the organization, however.

▶ *Risk tolerance.* A statement of the organization's risk tolerance should be included for the benefit of the team. This is difficult to quantify, however. Some of the quantification/qualification techniques will prove useful in analyzing risk tolerance. Risk tolerance is also fluid; it is impacted by many outside influences, such as the economy.

> **Risk tolerance: Just how much heat can you stand?**

▶ *Risk plan template.* Similar to management policies, the template guides the team through the process. You should develop a spreadsheet that has areas for the various categories of risk, risks identified in those categories, your team's assessment of those risks, and what steps are planned to handle the risks. Keep the development of such a spreadsheet in mind as you read the rest of this chapter, where I will explain what each of these means. You might find it useful to use the work breakdown structure (see below) as a tool to develop project risks.

▶ *Work breakdown structure.* The WBS provides a framework of all of the activities necessary to complete the project.

Risk Management Plan

The outcome of the risk management planning process will be the plan itself. It will define how the rest of the process will proceed. Further steps—identification, analysis, and response—will be structured based on the risk management plan.

Some of the typical topics in the plan include:

▶ *Techniques.* The methods of identification and analysis that will be used.

▶ *Roles and responsibilities.* Who does what for a given process. There may be modifications to the organization's traditional duties. Specialized analysis may be assigned to those outside of the project team if that is where the expertise lies.

▶ *Budgeting and schedule.* If the organization requires, a separate budget and schedule can be established for the exercise.

▶ *Evaluation of the results.* It is valuable to establish the criteria for evaluating the outputs of the exercises so that a consistent approach will be used. Thresholds should also be identified so that the organization's risk tolerance can be taken into account.

▶ *Reporting and tracking.* Protocols should be developed to provide for timely documentation and dissemination of the information generated in the process.

Risk Assessment

The subcategories of risk assessment have to do with assessing what risks might be encountered, deciding just how bad each might be, and developing a plan to deal with each. Specifically, the steps are:

1. *Risk identification.* Determining likely risks that may impact the project and determining the particular details of each.

2. *Risk quantification and qualification.* These are objective and subjective methods for evaluating the risks. Bear in mind that risks are interactive; that is to say that a schedule risk event will likely impact cost, scope, and quality, and could also have an effect on staffing if the delay changes rotation dates for some team members.

3. *Risk response planning.* Once the assessment exercise is complete, you have to develop plans and procedures to handle those risks that

What are the risks?
And what are they
like?

you have decided to respond to. Remember that you will likely decide to ignore some risks, either because they are too remote or you
lack the ability or resources to control them.

4. *Risk monitoring and control.* You have the responsibility to develop a
    monitoring scheme so that you can track your response plan through-
    out the project. This should include the requirement to revisit the risk
    management plan periodically as the project goes forward.

Risk Identification

Risk identification is a continuing exercise in which you determine the risks
that may impact the project and define the characteristics of each. Risk
identification should be done during the initiating process to estimate the
potential for project success. At this stage, numerous potential risks may
cause the project to be canceled or seriously modified.

Risks at this early stage can relate to the project itself and to the product
that the project will deliver. For example, the very best planned and executed
project will be a failure if the product delivered does not perform or has no
market. Conversely, a poorly run project may deliver a product that performs well but has insufficient time in its lifecycle and eventually becomes
an economic failure.

Risk Identification Inputs   The tools that you have at your disposal will
greatly affect the quality of the risk identification exercise. The more the
team knows about the product and the environment in which the project is

being conducted, the better they will be able to assess the risks involved. Following are several potential inputs to the risk identification exercise.

The beginning of the risk identification exercise is the development of the risk management plan, as I described above.

What the project is going to produce relates to the nature of the product itself and how it impacts risk. Projects that produce products using unknown or adventuresome technology are inherently more risky than those using proven technology. Similarly, projects that develop "serial number one" entail more risk than building the next McDonald's restaurant.

Decisions from other planning processes and organizations can seriously impact your part of the project. Risk assessment cannot be done in a vacuum. Outputs from the other knowledge areas (scope, schedule, cost, etc.) need to be systematically reviewed to assess their potential impact on the process. Examples of this exercise might be a review of the procurement plan. If your procurement plan is driven by an aggressive schedule, it might entail a lot of cost plus or other types of reimbursable contracts. By their very open-ended nature, reimbursable contracts are more risky. However, if time to market for the product is a prime consideration, then the risk may well be worthwhile.

The amount of information available when the cost estimate is assembled certainly will be reflected in the risk involved in the cost of the job. Your experience and knowledge of the steps needed to carry out the plan also is a consideration. This, tied to the staffing plan, can generate significant risks to the project. It might be that the knowledge to carry out the project rests in one person. The project may be so novel that there is no known precedent that can be used for guidance.

Your organization may be striving for a level of quality that has not been achieved before. You may not be able to rely on business-as-usual skills to reach that standard.

Archived information can be used if the project is repetitive, such as installing a new computer program at yet another branch bank. The historical project files will be invaluable in defining risks that may be encountered. Even if the files are incomplete, assigning staff from previous similar projects would help.

To benchmark the quality of the project estimate, the use of commercial and other databases should be used. In this way, oversights or an overzealous estimator can be exposed and the cost risks identified.

You need to be mindful of the many **risk categories** that exist. Risk identification should be global in nature, and concentrate on the internal (or micro) risks as well as the external (or macro) risks. The above discussion relates primarily to internal risks, but the external risks are equally important and in many cases more difficult to mitigate. For example, government regulations relating to the product itself need to be identified. Agencies such as the Consumer Products Safety Commission have rules that can seriously impact the product generated by the project.

Copyright and patent implications exist. Various authorities will regulate the project. Such a simple task as installing a driveway from a county road will involve a curb cut permit, which may take weeks to get. This needs to be identified in the activity analysis that goes into generating a schedule.

Generally, risks can be concentrated in two areas:

▶ *Business risk.* These are the risks inherent in the conduct of the project. For example, the risk that the estimate is wrong or that you do not have adequate skill to run the project.

▶ *Pure risk.* These are insurable risks, such as disasters, warranties, and other events that can be mitigated by money.

Risks should also be categorized as predictable or not. This is commonly thought of as knowns, known-unknowns, and unknown-unknowns. The first are those risks that you are aware of and feel will impact you. An example might be a planned absence of one of your team members. You know it is going to happen and you know it will affect the labor on your job.

A known-unknown is a situation that you know is going to happen, but are unsure if the situation will involve you. This might be the expiration of the plant labor agreement. It is sure to happen, but you don't know if your contractors will honor a picket line.

Unknown-unknowns cannot be analyzed, because there is no way to know they exist until they happen. They are handled by a method called *workarounds*, which I will discuss later.

Risk Identification Methods (Tools and Techniques)   You can use a number of techniques to identify and characterize risks. However, for them to be effective, you should formalize them and use them as a standard method on all projects. In this way their use will become second nature, and all project team members will become familiar with them and understand their value.

Some tools and techniques called out in the PMBOK are:

▶ *Information gathering techniques.* In order to be efficient in the process, various information gathering techniques should be used. These include brainstorming, in which the team gathers to dissect the project to find problem areas, seeking expert judgment form those inside or outside the organization, and conducting some of the analysis techniques, such as a SWOT (strengths, weaknesses, opportunities, and threats) exercise to assess the current status of the project and organization.

▶ *Checklists.* Checklists should be used at all stages of the project to ensure that needed items are covered before the next stage begins. They can be general and apply to a variety of situations, such as checking the estimate for completeness. This sort of checklist would explore whether all costs had been accounted for, including indirect costs, which are often omitted or underestimated. In the case of construction projects, indirect costs such as the contractor's profit and overhead, his statutory obligations of FICA withholding, State and Federal Unemployment Insurance, and the owner's costs of travel and living, engineering, taxes, and freight can easily be 40 percent of the direct costs of equipment and the material and labor to install it. Forcing a review of the estimate and testing it against commercial databases and earlier projects should uncover any errors.

Checklists can also be very specific. In the construction example the checklist could be used to ensure that all wiring has termination numbers assigned, or that all valves have identification tags.

Some examples of checklists that can be of value include technology issues relating to the product being produced, the safety and environmental aspects of the project and the product, governmental and community affairs issues, skill assessments of the team members, input from all levels of the organization concerning utility and maintenance of equipment or processes, and other areas of concern.

Obviously, the checklists used at the beginning of a project will vary greatly from those used later. A self-assessment early on—such as, do we *really* know what we want?—will differ from a procurement checklist, the purpose of which is to make sure you have all the bases covered in a contract.

▶ *Flowcharting.* Flowcharting can be used at all stages of the

project and shares many of the characteristics of checklists. In

this sense, flowcharting

is the technique of ask-

ing a yes/no question

> **Flowcharting: A feedback-based management method**

about an item and programming the response to be a predeter-

mined step. As an example, the question could be asked, "Is

the execution plan acceptable to all parties?" The "yes" re-

sponse would lead to "Execute plan." The "no" response could

be "Review and revise plan."

▶ *Interviewing.* One difficulty that many projects encounter is the

lack of input from key players and others who possess knowl-

edge that the project team needs. For example, there will always

be legal issues. These may entail permitting for a new or revised

facility, or copyright and patent considerations. There could be

other regulatory items. It would be prudent for you to interview

the legal staff during the planning stage, and again during execu-

tion, to identify and control these potential risks. Legal is but

one example. Risk-oriented interviews should be conducted with

any and all groups and stakeholders to determine unknowns in

the project. Every unknown is a risk! Records of the interviews

should be a part of the project file and should be re-examined

during the formal project review process.

The PMBOK also describes the Delphi technique, a method that uses experts unrelated to the project to analyze it for risks. A facilitator interviews the experts, who are anonymous to you and the team. The logic here is that no one with an axe to grind will have undue influence over the results.

The Result of Risk Identification (Outputs)   Once the risks have been identified they must be made known. Bear in mind that you will repeat the process of risk identification during later stages of the project; new risks will be identified, and some old risks will drop off the list.

There are generally three outputs identified in the PMBOK:

The Risks Themselves

Sources of risk. These will be the general areas that can generate risks, not specifically identified events. For example, poor estimating might be a general class of identified risk. No specific instance of poor estimating has been identified. A flag has simply been raised that the estimate might be suspect. This would be especially important in the case of a project to develop new technology. Ironically, it would also be true in the example of a new McDonald's restaurant, even though many have been built before. Precisely for this reason, profit margins on these types of projects are very low, and minor estimating errors can spell disaster.

Other sources of risk might be the potential for design errors and omissions, a poor definition and understanding of the roles and responsibilities of team members, an overestimation of the skills of the project team, or the potential for changes in the product requirements over the life of the project.

Note that no specific deficiency has been identified in this category. Rather, this is a listing of potential areas of risk.

Potential risk events. These are discrete items that have been identified, as opposed to the general areas found above. As an example, natural disasters or a change in government regulations would be discrete events. These would trigger specific mitigation plans to be carried out in the event they occurred.

These potential risk events can be very specific to a type of project. Weather disasters will impact a construction project much more than they will software implementation.

Both sources of risk and potential risk events should ultimately be characterized in terms of probability, possible outcomes, and the timing or frequency of occurrence. For example, the expiration of a labor contract would be a source of risk that would be known both in probability (it is going to happen) and in timing (it is a certain date). Possible outcomes can be identified with a high degree of accuracy, based on past history. In this case, outcomes might be a strike, a new contract, or continuation of the old contract. It is interesting to note here that the potential for higher labor cost due to this event forms an estimating risk, while the prospect of a strike or other labor action constitutes a schedule risk. Based on history, it would have been a judgment call whether or not to include them in the plan.

Risk Symptoms or Triggers

PMBOK defines risk symptoms as triggers that are indirect indications of an impending risk. In the labor contract example above, absenteeism, vandalism, and poor quality requiring rework would be early indications that the expiration of the contract would not go smoothly. (As an aside, most major construction projects develop a "project agreement" whereby the unions and contractors agree in advance on how to handle a contract dispute or expiration. There is typically an up-front monetary incentive for labor harmony.)

> **Indirect indications of problems are called "risk triggers"**

Other examples of triggers are overspending early in the project as a trigger to a poor estimate, or falling behind as an indicator of a poor schedule. These can be exposed using earned value analysis, described in Chapter 7.

Modification to Other Areas or Processes

As mentioned early in this discussion, risk is at once a PMBOK process and an input to other PMBOK processes. The sources of risk regarding estimating and scheduling may lead to a reassessment of the quality and completeness of the work breakdown schedule (WBS), as an example.

Risk Quantification and Qualification

Once the risks are identified at a given stage of the project, you must quantify or assess them to see which need to be planned for and which will be accepted if they occur. The PMBOK has recently changed to address quantification, or objective, methods separately from qualification, or subjective, ones. This chapter addresses them in tandem because the two are often used together and are certainly interrelated.

As an example, a schedule risk caused by the departure of a key team member would likely

> **Qualification means "subjective"**
> **Quantification means "objective"**

warrant a plan in case it happens, while a comet hitting the building would not. It is important to realize that every project has risks, as does every human activity, and some of them simply cannot be mitigated but must be accepted. Also, to attempt to quantify and mitigate every risk would lead to the project team doing nothing else—the ultimate risk! This is known as "analysis paralysis." In addition, remember that risk quantification deals with what-ifs, and this is not a precise science. The use of mathematical techniques is a powerful tool in assessing risk, but its precision depends on the accuracy of the input. This perception of precision may lead to a false sense of well-being. As is said in the computer age "Garbage in; gospel out."

Risk quantification is the process of assessing the impact of a given risk on the project, and developing and analyzing the possible outcomes on the project. This exercise is really a way of determining which of the identified risks deserve to have plans developed to mitigate (or enhance, in the case of positive risks or opportunities) their effect on the project.

This exercise is further complicated because the project is not a single item. Even the simplest of projects has the three basic building blocks of a scope, an estimate, and a schedule, a characteristic shared by even the most complex projects. A problem in one of these areas will almost always have an impact on one or both of the others. A change in scope caused by any number of factors will generally have an impact on cost, and may well affect schedule as well. Cost concerns may cause schedule delays. Schedule delays will always impact cost.

Quantification can be a difficult task. Just remember to concentrate on the risks that either have the greatest impact or for which a mitigation plan can be developed. Don't concern yourself with earthquakes or tidal waves!

Risk Quantification and Qualification Inputs   As risk quantification is a continuance of risk identification, the tools will naturally derive from the identification process. These are described below.

Sources of risk. The listing of the sources of risk developed during risk identification will form the basis of the analysis during risk quantification. There needs to be a one-to-one relationship, with an assessment for each identified risk. This might be as simple as recognition that the estimate should be checked before going forward.

Potential risk events. Since these tend to be discrete activities, such as a key player leaving, specific outcomes should be developed. These outcomes might vary depending on where the project stands at the time. A designer leaving after the design is complete is not as critical as one leaving in the middle of the development effort.

Scope documents. Poorly written scopes are the primary cause of cost and schedule problems. This section could even be expanded to include the mission, vision, and strategy statements that should have been developed before the project was even started. A popular contention is that projects fail at the strategy stage. Not everyone understands or agrees with what is to be done. This is further exacerbated by an unwillingness to appear to not understand what is proposed.

Cost estimates. Cost estimates are a major area of risk and need to be used during assessment.

Schedules. During risk analysis, the durations assigned in the scheduling phase will have to be studied to determine potential outcomes if the durations vary from the plan.

Risk tolerance. An intangible needed for the risk quantification exercise is a baseline by which to judge riskiness. Therefore, an additional input into the calculation is risk tolerance. A primary concern during risk quantification is how, exactly, the collective organization views risk. Some organizations have a very high risk tolerance and just roll with the punches when things don't go as planned. Perhaps there is another budget that can be tapped to cover cost overruns. It is possible that the schedule could be delayed without serious implications. On the other hand, perhaps the plant manager's job (and maybe yours) is on the line if this project is late or goes over budget.

As was seen earlier, risk tolerance is one of the inputs into the risk management plan. Recall, however, that the risk management plan was developed at the outset. Now that the initial risk identification exercise has been completed, management's risk tolerance may have changed. It likely will remain fluid throughout the project. Therefore, as you revisit the entire risk exercise at later stages in the project, recalibration of the organization's risk tolerance will be necessary. Even when the project is almost complete and the risks encountered have been handled, you must not let down your guard. This is especially true if the project is getting close to the spending limit or milestone date.

Risk Quantification and Qualification Methods (Tools and Techniques)

There are a great many analytical tools available for assessing risk. Remember, however, that these are only tools, and that your judgment will be critical if the exercise is to be meaningful. There also exist techniques for thinking through a problem or situation that do not involve statistical techniques. Often the risks identified do not lend themselves to hard analysis. You might not have the background in analytical techniques, and also may better understand these "soft" tools. Finally, as mentioned previously, analytical techniques can produce a false sense of well being because of their authoritative nature. The statistical methods generally require large populations of data to be valid. Not only might such a population be unavailable, the results derived when using smaller sample sizes can be downright wrong! Also, let's understand that this is not a treatment of statistical analysis—the discussion of statistical methods will be descriptive in nature and the coverage will not be exhaustive. Further detail can be obtained by referencing a text on the subject.

I want to begin with a review of some of the analytical methods, and then go on to the less objective techniques.

Objective Methods (Quantification)

Sensitivity analysis. This involves assigning every practical value to the item in question and seeing how each impacts the final cost or duration of the project. Those that can vary by a wide margin and still have only a minimal impact on the outcome should be rank lower than others that cause more variation.

Expected monetary value (EMV). As a tool for assessment, expected monetary value is the product of two numbers:

1. The risk event probability.
2. The value of the event.

The risk event probability is an estimate of the likelihood that the event will occur. The value of the event is the loss or gain that will result *if* the event occurs.

The use of expected monetary value will allow the event's risk to be compared to the organization's risk tolerance. Risk tolerance is a function of the relative impact that the risk carries.

Expected monetary value is the product of two numbers:
- **The risk event probability**
- **The value of the event**

As an illustration, suppose that two organizations are going to build new restaurants. Further suppose that the two sites selected used to be gas stations with buried tanks that will have to be removed, and the soil condition is currently unknown. It has been estimated that the cost to clean up the site after the tanks are removed could be as high as $100,000.

The risk event value is $100,000. The risk event probability is between 0 percent and 100 percent. Let's assume for the sake of argument that the probability is 75 percent, meaning that we believe some cleanup will be necessary but we won't have to dig to the center of the earth. Therefore, the EMV is $75,000 ($100,000 × .75). It does not mean that is all it will cost; we might be unlucky. On the other hand, it may cost little or nothing. It is a judgment call.

$$\text{Expected Monetary Value}$$
$$=$$
$$\text{Impact} \times \text{Probability}$$

How does this relate to risk tolerance? Suppose the two organizations were McDonald's and Burger King. Suppose they were McDonald's and Uncle Harry's Hamburgers. The EMV has to be looked at through the spyglass of tolerance. McDonald's and Burger King likely would not care. Uncle Harry might cancel the project.

Bear in mind that the effects of the expected monetary value can be cumulative. You could easily have a number of risks that could be analyzed by EMV. While any one in itself might not be a deal killer, the combined impact could be such that it would exceed the organization's risk tolerance. The cumulative nature can be demonstrated by the use of a decision tree analysis, assuming that one decision on risk affects another decision on a subsequent risk. This may not be the case in all projects. It may be that the risks identified can be considered discrete unto themselves. A combination of risk interactions will most likely be the norm.

Decision tree analysis. The use of a decision tree involves choosing between alternative actions and then assigning a probability and value to each, as was done in expected monetary value. Then a series of "what ifs" or alternative outcomes are generated, and their EMVs are assigned.

This can go on for many steps. However, at some point the analysis gets so unwieldy, and the assumptions so unsupportable, that the analysis fails to be of value.

Choosing between alternate projects is a common use of the decision tree. Once the alternate plans are identified, a range of probable outcomes for each can be assumed, and the value of each assigned. Subsequent actions are then assigned for each of these outcomes, and further assumptions made and their outcomes estimated. When finished, the optimal solution(s) can be ascertained.

Once this is done, you would be wise to vary your assumptions (see sensitivity analysis above) to test just how robust the result is. If you get a different solution when you vary the inputs, you need to test your as-

Always
test
your
assumptions

sumptions. Generally, the result may flip-flop between two courses of action. This is where your judgment comes in. You may need to go to the project sponsor for an answer!

In the example shown in Figure 11.1, I analyze two ways to obtain a computer to be used as a point-of-sale machine for a retail business. I have researched the market and concluded that I can buy a new one for $2,000, or a used one for $1,000. These are known as the *decision defini-tion* and the *decision cost*.

Next there is a *chance node*. This is where you make your judgment as to the likelihood of each of two possible outcomes. In my example, I have assigned a 90 percent probability that a new computer will work correctly. This leaves a 10 percent chance that it will not. For the used machine, I have assigned a 60 percent chance that it will work and a 40 percent chance that it will not. Note that the total must equal 100 percent because the two outcomes are mutually exclusive.

Finally, I have to assign a monetary value to the two possibilities. I have chosen $1,500 in sales if the computer works, and $500 in sales if it does not. This is because poor service will turn customers away.

Once this tree is filled out, I can calculate the *branch value* for each of the two branches, New and Used. This is done by changing the sign of the cost and adding to this amount algebraically to the sum of the two probabilities times their respective monetary values. In my example, the math looks like this:

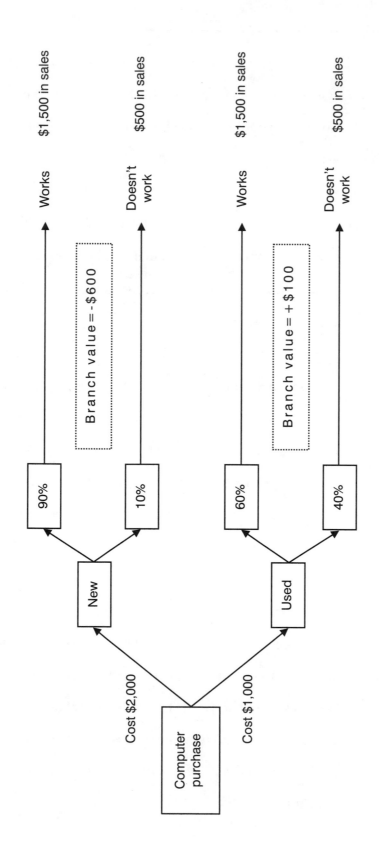

Figure 11.1   Decision Tree Example

New   (–\$2,000) + (.90 × \$1,500) + (.10 × \$500)) = -\$600

Used   (–\$1,000) + (.60 × \$1,500) + (.40 × \$500)) = +\$100

Therefore, you can see that I would be better off buying the used computer and taking the risk that it will not work correctly. In order to better understand this concept, I suggest that you vary the numbers above to see how the results change. You may find that the branch value for both choices goes positive. Or both could go negative, in which case you would question the wisdom of the decision in the first place.

Simulations. The use of simulations involves running a set of variables in all practical combinations to develop a most likely result. The most common application in project management is for the testing of schedule durations and dependencies, although they can be used on cost estimates as well.

The model generally used is the Monte Carlo simulation, named after the famed casino in Monaco. The two have in common the fact that they are dealing with a great number of variable and possible values for those variables.

In a schedule simulation, the Monte Carlo approach performs the project thousands of times, using the network diagram developed during schedule preparation. Each time one or more possible durations and/or dependencies are varied, while others are held constant. All of the possible outcomes are plotted, and the process generates the most likely final outcome. You can establish certain parameters as unchangeable to see the impact of decisions regarding work schedules and dependencies that result in different critical paths through the schedule.

Performing the Monte Carlo method requires the use of computer software. (The amount of time and effort to do otherwise is too great.) There are a number of stand-alone programs, as well as add-ins to existing spreadsheets, that can be acquired to perform the simulation.

The output of a Monte Carlo schedule simulation is a distribution or S-curve representing the cumulative probability of a completing a project by a given time. You and your team can analyze the summary data and select a point on the curve that represents the proper schedule of the project based on risk tolerance. Just as important, Monte Carlo also identifies path convergence, which is where the arrows converge on a single task from several paths. This task will therefore have a higher risk assigned to it, since it impacts several paths through the schedule. An example might be a shutdown milestone for the installation of a network. All actors on the project have to perform efficiently in order to make the date.

For example, let's assume that the Monte Carlo simulation showed that the project could be done in as few as 45 days, or as many as 89 days. In such a case, 45 days would represent the zero percentile (nearly impossible), while 89 would be the 100th percentile (virtually guaranteed). How could you use this information to decide on an overall duration? A typical approach would be to establish a confidence level during the project plan development; for instance, "We will accept the 90th percentile of a schedule simulation as our duration." Of course, you would need to dissect the schedule generated at that confidence level to be able to track the project in the future. In this case, the duration might be around 80 days.

Large, complex projects benefit most from the use of this type of simulation. Even then accuracy depends on the underlying assumptions. A cost simulation would represent dollars versus likelihood.

PERT. Program evaluation and review technique, (or PERT) is a scheduling development method used to assess the risk inherent in the schedule. PERT allows you to assign optimistic, most likely, and pessimistic durations to a given activity. The calculation then provides an expected value for the activity. In many cases, this will be different than the most likely. A more complete treatment of PERT can be found in Chapter 6.)

Subjective Methods (Qualification)   The next area of risk assessment is the nonmathematical one. This suggests that risk likelihood falls on a continuum from rare to commonplace, and that risk impact similarly would run from severe to minimal. While subjective analysis cannot be defended on a purely statistical basis, it is probably used more on projects that the other methods. It suffers from a lack of concrete evidence to back up the assumptions made—in many cases, the necessary data may be unavailable. Therefore it is readily open to challenge. It requires the input of

The PMBOK describes what it calls "expert judgment"

experienced and qualified team members. The PMBOK describes this as "expert judgment."

Also, since these analyses are not mathematically calculable, they are measured by either an ordinal scale (low, medium, or high) or a cardinal scale that assigns numbers (for example, .1,.3,.5,.7,.9) to the ordinal terms.

There are, however, tools available to assess risks on a project when the analytic approach is not used. Remember that risk analysis, with its subsets of identification, quantification, qualification, control planning, and plan execution, should be done at various stages of the project.

SWOT. This stands for strengths, weaknesses, opportunities, and threats. It is an organized way of looking at the project and project team and providing an assessment of the situation at a given point in time. This process is outlined as follows:

- ▶ *Strengths:* What strengths do we have, and how can we take advantage of them?

- ▶ *Weaknesses:* What weaknesses do we have, and how can we minimize their impact on the project?

- ▶ *Opportunities:* What opportunities are there, and how can we capitalize on them?

- ▶ *Threats:* What threats to the project exist? What can we do to eliminate or minimize them?

Since this text is dealing with risk, the two categories of weaknesses and threats will be explored further.

Weaknesses are important because they represent a chance for things to go bad and are internally generated. The ultimate weakness is that the project team members are incompetent and do not know what they are doing. Plans should be made to overcome personnel weaknesses by supplying training or other means to mitigate the impact of such shortcomings. Other means could be assigning different or additional personnel to the project, or hiring consultants to handle the aspects of the project that the team is incapable of doing. This is common in complex engineering and software projects.

Threats, on the other hand, can be viewed as being somewhat beyond the control of the project team. This does not mean they cannot be handled, but rather that their source is either an outside influence or the organization itself. This could be because someone in the company does not buy into the project strategy or has some other hidden agenda that can jeopardize the project.

The outcome of a SWOT analysis would be a tabulation of the threats and weaknesses identified, and the relative importance of each. Some notion as to the degree of influence you have over each would also be of value.

Force field analysis. In a force field analysis, the project team concentrates on the actions of people and groups that have a negative impact on the project. This is a difficult exercise to quantify, and therefore is best done by attempting to find ways to accommodate or neutralize the resistance. In the case where someone in a position of authority over the project has strong objections to some aspect of the plan, the strategy will likely be to modify the plan to suit the individual. Remember that project management in any organization is not a popularity contest, nor is the project environment a democracy. If someone on the project team can't accept this, then perhaps they have missed their calling.

Other areas to concentrate on when performing a force field analysis could include the feelings or perceptions of other groups not directly related to the project. Perhaps the project will have the potential for noxious emissions. While the necessary permits may be obtainable, the support of the local community will need to be taken into account.

Maybe a lot of extra car and truck traffic will occur during the project, and perhaps beyond. In this case, the community as well as their elected leaders will have a say whether you plan for it or not.

The Results of Risk Quantification and Qualification (Outputs)   The purpose of the exercise of risk quantification is to assess each identified risk and make a judgment about the result of its occurring. Therefore, the list developed needs to be characterized so that you will know what to do about each. This characterization falls into two general categories, active and passive. In this exercise, positive risks (opportunities) will have been analyzed as well and will be included in the output.

- ▶ Opportunities to pursue
- ▶ Threats to respond to
- ▶ Opportunities to ignore
- ▶ Threats to accept

The logic behind the resulting list should be documented so that you can keep focused. This listing will also form the basis of the next step, which is to develop a risk response control plan.

Developing a Risk Response Control Plan   Now that the risks have been identified and quantified (a process also referred to as "risk assessment" in earlier versions of the PMBOK), it is time for you to develop a plan on how to handle the risks that have been chosen for action. Remember that in the quantification/qualification output discussion we stated that there would be risks to respond to and those to accept. You will need to develop plans for the former should they occur.

There are generally four ways to handle risks:

▶ *Avoidance.* You can avoid the risk. This means finding its root cause, using the exercises above, and eliminating it. For example, suppose that there was a risk of unfavorable community relations due to an industrial installation near a neighborhood. This actually happened in one mill town, and the company avoided the problem by offering to purchase residents' houses for twice the appraised value. Those homeowners who had objected accepted the offer and moved.

▶ *Transference or deflection.* Transference involves getting someone else to accept the responsibility for the risk and the response to that risk. You should bear in mind that transference does not eliminate the risk. It is still there; it is just someone else's duty to handle it. It generally involves a payment of some kind, such as an extra payment in a contract or special insurance.

▶ *Mitigation.* The risk can be mitigated, or its influence lessened. Reducing the probability that the risk will occur—perhaps through changes in the product description—or augmenting staffing can accomplish this. You also could reduce the risk event value by buying insurance against the risk, obtaining war-

ranties, or bonding suppliers and contractors if the risk is that of
a default on a contract.

▶ *Acceptance.* It is a viable strategy to take the approach that the
risk will be accepted if it occurs. This approach should be cou-
pled with a "what if?" plan to execute if the risk occurs. You
need to establish some sort of reserve or contingency allowance
to fund the "what if?" approach. As an example, certain weather
events *could* happen, so the most logical approach might be for
you to accept the fact that they *will* happen and plan for them.
This might involve a plan for securing a construction site in case
of a hurricane. However, you would not expect a contractor to
secure the site each afternoon. He might be perfectly happy to
do it, but you don't want to pay for it.

Risk Response Development Inputs   The inputs to risk response development are the outputs of the quantification process. Namely:

▶ Threats to respond to

▶ Threats to accept

Risk Response Development Methods (Tools and Techniques)   Once
the threats are identified and characterized, specific plans can be developed
to handle them. Some that may be used are:

▶ Scope, estimate, and schedule development discipline. In many
organizations, discipline in the development of project documents

in almost nonexistent. It is of great value to enforce a disciplined approach to developing these items in an organized and consistent fashion. It is inconceivable that someone would think that they could produce an estimate without a scope, but it happens all the time. People will pull a cost out of thin air when pressed for an answer, without regard for all of the elements involved in the project. Likewise, it strains the imagination that a schedule can be done without an estimate; the estimate is the only reliable source of man-hours to be expended, which is the key to developing durations.

▶ The use of development checklists should be required for all stages of project development. The use of these checklists should be viewed as a positive exercise. No one can be expected to remember everything at once.

▶ Change management procedures. If you expect that there will be pressure for scope changes, a formal scope-change procedure should be put into effect. If you *don't* expect any pressure for scope changes, a formal scope-change procedure still should be put into effect! For there will *always* be pressure for scope changes!

What is the number one reason for pressure for scope changes? Lousy scopes. See the two items above.

What can be said for scope changes can be said for schedule changes. Cost changes, on the other hand, tend to be a little subtler. One common pitfall in estimates is the use of allowances. Allowances imply no scope. The scope is whatever the user of the allowance thinks it is. Avoid allowances, especially when someone else is going to spend them.

▶ Contingency plans can be developed to cover eventualities.

▶ Alternative strategies are similar to contingency plans, except that they are proactive instead of reactive. That is to say that the risk identified can be handled "if" it happens (contingency), or plans can be made to avoid its happening (avoidance). One such alternate strategy might be to buy from a more reliable source. Of course, the downside is that the new source might be more expensive. You might find a decision tree analysis useful here.

▶ Insurance can be purchased to cover risks that cannot be handled in any other practical way. This would include bonding contractors and suppliers as well as disaster insurance, business interruption, and other forms of indemnification.

The Results of Risk Response Development (Outputs)

▶ *Risk management plan.* The most obvious output from the exercise of risk response development is the risk management plan, which should document the identification and quantification exercises, and identify risks to be responded to if they occur as well as those that have been accepted.

The plan should designate the parties responsible for each of its elements, the actions to be taken, and the triggers for these actions. For instance, the purchasing agent might be responsible for initiating the bonding process for contractors upon receiving bids that indicate the risk of default is higher than the organization is willing to accept. Likewise, the facility manager would make the call if severe weather were predicted.

The risk management plan should also be used in the earlier stages of a project to act upon deviations. In the early stages of engineering, earned value analysis should be conducted to see if significant deviations from the spending curve are occurring. Purchase price versus budget should be tracked.

The risk management plan can be divided into contingency plans ("what if?") and alternative action plans that can be carried out if deviations occur that dictate that a whole new project plan be implemented. In this way, contingency plans might be considered a micro approach (i.e., hire a consultant to cover the project manager's absence), while alternative action plans might be considered a macro approach (i.e., reschedule the project to a more favorable time).

▶ Establish reserves. Reserves are funds set aside to cover events that may occur (also called contingency and escalation or management reserves). Obviously, funds for events that will occur should be covered in the base budget. A reserve of 10 percent is not unusual. Contingency should not be used for scope changes. Escalation should be established to cover cost increases caused by inflation, and are expected to be spent over the duration of the project.

Other types of reserves might be padding the schedule with longer than expected durations, and staffing the job with more resources than are absolutely needed to allow for personnel problems. Both of these techniques are legitimate if they arc done out in the open—which they generally are not.

Risk Response Control　　　Risk response control involves executing the risk management plan as events unfold. More than that, however, the plan should contain a feedback mechanism whereby the entire planning cycle is reviewed to see if the event will impact other aspects of the plan. Remember that the impact may be positive or negative. Consider that schedule delays might actually help get an otherwise critical piece of equipment on site before it can have an adverse effect. Also, different subcontracting methods, such as lump sum, could be used that would shift the risk to someone other than the owner. Risk response control inputs include:

▶ The risk management plan

▶ The risk event that occurs

▶ Continuing assessment of the risks inherent in the project

The Results of Risk Response Control (Outputs)   The triggering of the risk response control plan will generate the appropriate outputs that were developed during the risk management process. As such, they will be actions that you deemed proper at the time of the exercise. However, in order for you to implement the plan effectively, you

> **A workaround is a plan developed to handle a risk that was unforeseen during the risk assessment**

must recognize that no plan is perfect; you must remain vigilant and ready to confront unanticipated risks for which you have no response plan in place. Reactions to such eventualities are known as *workarounds*. When these occur you need to analyze the entire plan to determine the influence of the unexpected event on the project. You should also try to determine if the unexpected event could have been foreseen had the risk analysis been more thorough.

CONCLUSION

This treatment of risk management is intended to cover the subject in a manner consistent with the PMBOK. This is because most project team members are unfamiliar with the concept as covered by PMI and might be at a disadvantage when preparing for the certification exam.

That said, reading the risk chapter in the PMBOK is recommended to further applicants' understanding of the concepts and vocabulary.

AREAS OF EMPHASIS IN THIS CHAPTER

The following are some of the key elements covered in this chapter and in the PMBOK:

- ▶ The elements of risk management (memorize these!)
  - Risk management planning (includes risk tolerance)
  - Risk identification
  - Qualitative risk analysis
  - Quantitative risk analysis
  - Risk response planning
  - Risk monitoring and control
- ▶ Remember the "inputs/tools and techniques/outputs" from the PMBOK format to help keep track of things
- ▶ Risk categories
  - Technical, quality, and performance risks
  - Project management risks
  - Organizational risks
  - External risks
- ▶ Risk identification techniques
  - Document review
  - Brainstorming

- Delphi technique

- Interviewing

- SWOT method

- Checklists

- Assumptions analysis

- Flowcharting

▶ Qualitative techniques

  - Probability/impact matrix

  - Ordinal and cardinal rankings

  - SWOT analysis

  - Force field analysis

▶ Quantitative techniques

  - Sensitivity analysis

  - Expected monetary value

  - Decision tree analysis

  - Simulations (Monte Carlo)

  - PERT

▶ Risk responses

  - Avoidance

  - Transference or deflection

  - Mitigation

  - Acceptance

✓ Contingency plan

✓ Reserves

✓ Fallback plan

▶ **Risk monitoring and control**

- Workarounds

- Change requests

- Feedback into risk management plan and response plans

CHAPTER ELEVEN SAMPLE QUESTIONS—SELECT THE *BEST* ANSWER

1. If a project has a 25 percent chance of a loss of $50,000 and a 75 percent chance of a profit of $100,000, what is the expected monetary value (EMV) of the project?

    A. A $75,000 profit

    B. A $12,500 loss

    C. A $62,500 profit

    D. A $ 50,000 loss

2. What is a workaround?

    A. An attempt to sneak additional scope into the project

    B. A solution or reaction to an unexpected occurrence

    C. The same thing as a contingency reserve

    D. Not defined

3. What is risk tolerance?

    A. A measure of an organization's willingness to accept risk

    B. Management's reaction when the unexpected occurs

    C. The ability of the project team to identify risks

    D. A qualitative measurement method

4. Which of the following is *not* a risk response mechanism?

    A. Avoidance

    B. Mitigation

    C.   Transference

    D.   Simulation

5.   What is decision tree analysis?

    A.   A simulation

    B.   A probabilistic method of predicting outcomes

    C.   Part of the PERT system

    D.   A risk response method

6.   When is the earliest that a thorough risk analysis can be done?

    A.   At project inception

    B.   After the work breakdown structure has been completed

    C.   During the Monte Carlo simulation

    D.   At the contracting/procurement stage

7.   Which of the following is *not* one of the PMBOK risk processes?

    A.   Risk response planning

    B.   Risk identification

    C.   Quantitative risk analysis

    D.   Risk tolerance control

8.   A Monte Carlo simulation is an example of:

    A.   A qualitative analysis method.

    B.   A quantitative analysis method

    C.   A type of risk response

    D.   A mitigation strategy

9. In a decision tree analysis, a branch has a cost of $300, a 65 percent chance of a $900 return, and a 35 percent chance of a $200 return. What is the value of that branch?

A. $900

B. $800

C. $355

D. $585

10. What are management reserves?

A. Funds to account for "known unknowns"

B. Funds to account for "unknown unknowns"

C. A method of risk avoidance

D. A workaround

Management reserves:
A. Funds to account for "known unknowns"
B. Funds to account for "unknown unknowns"
C. A method of risk avoidance
D. A workaround

11. What is the objective of risk identification?

    A. Identify the person who has the responsibility for the project

    B. Expose risks that may occur

    C. React to events that have occurred

    D. Quantify risks

12. If a risk has a 40 percent chance of occurring and the financial impact is $25,000, what is the result, and what is it called?

    A. $25,000; risk probability

    B. $15,000; risk reserve

    C. $10,000; expected monetary value

    D. $10,000; risk priority number

13. PERT is a scheduling technique that:

    A. Does not use precedence diagrams

    B. Analyzes schedules using uncertainty

    C. Is the same as CPM

    D. Runs multiple simulations to derive the final schedule

14. If you are analyzing a risk but lack numerical evidence as to its impact, you should:

    A. Ignore the risk until you can collect data

    B. Ask management for more time

    C. Use a quantitative method

    D. Use a qualitative method

15. You can transfer a risk by:

    A. Purchasing insurance

    B. Assigning more staff

    C. Revisiting the analysis of the risk

    D. Changing the organization's risk tolerance

16. Which of the following is *not* a quantitative method?

    A. SWOT

    B. Monte Carlo simulation

    C. Decision tree analysis

    D. Sensitivity analysis

17. Deciding to use a different strategy is an example of:

    A. Risk assessment

    B. Monte Carlo simulation

    C. Risk avoidance

    D. Risk quantification

18. What is a major shortcoming in the use of PERT?

    A. It is a very hard program to learn

    B. It is the same as CPM

    C. It is difficult to accurately identify the range of durations to use

    D. It is in very common use

19. Why should risk management be done?

A. It is part of the project methodology

B. Other team members expect it

C. It should only be done on large projects

D. To protect the project's success from uncertainty

20. Risks that are identified as having a minimal impact on the project should be:

A. Ignored

B. Identified in a memorandum to the end user

C. Documented and reassessed during periodic reviews

D. Handled by buying insurance

Chapter 12

Procurement

INTRODUCTION

Managing contracts in a project management environment is one of the knowledge areas defined in the PMBOK. While procurement activities occur routinely throughout the life of the organization, I will emphasize the activities needed to successfully manage the process in a project environment.

The general outline that this chapter will follow is the project procurement management chapter of the PMBOK. (This is Chapter 12 of the standard.) While we are concentrating on project procurement, the steps defined by PMBOK are universally applicable to any procurement process:

▶ *Procurement planning.* Deciding what to procure, and when it needs to be purchased to fit the project schedule.

▶ *Solicitation planning.* Developing the specifications and other requirements, and identifying potential "sellers" of the "product."

▶ *Solicitation.* The act of obtaining quotations and bids.

▶ *Source selection.* Developing the evaluation criteria and selecting a source.

▶ *Contract administration.* The activity that involves managing the relationship between the "buyer" and the "seller."

▶ *Contract closeout.* At the completion of the contract, finalizing payments and warranties, and resolving outstanding items.

As is the case with all project areas, the six processes of the procurement area are interactive and there is frequently no clearly defined boundary between them. Also, a typical project has many procurement activities going on at once, with each of them in different stages of development. Note that the steps above apply to ongoing operations as well; they are simply a logical way to handle the purchase of space shuttles or lawn care services. This way of thinking, and the discipline that it imposes on the process, will therefore be especially valuable for those that are part-time project people and part-time operations people.

PROCUREMENT PLANNING

Projects by their very nature consume resources to develop an end product. This is true whether the project is to build something concrete or to develop intellectual property, such as computer code. Procurement planning is the process of identifying

the items to be procured and deciding whether to obtain them from within the orga-

nization, or go outside. If the decision is to go outside, you must then decide or rec-

ommend sources, contract types, and a procurement schedule. Notice the use of the

word recommend. It is a rare project that gives a project manager total autonomy

over the procurement process. This is primarily due to the legal nature of the trans-

action. Few project managers are aware of the intricacies of contract law. This

course is no exception. What is learned here will make you wiser in the realm of con-

tract law, but will not be a substitute for legal competence or the use of the company

legal and contracts department.

Procurement planning consists of four distinct subtopics:

▶ What to procure

▶ To contract or not to contract . . . that is the question

▶ What type of contract to use

▶ Develop a procurement management plan for subcontracts

What to Procure

Deciding what to procure should

be simple, because you will have

> **What to procure is based on the work breakdown structure**

developed a work breakdown structure (WBS) down to the level needed to

develop an estimate. In this exercise, you would have identified everything

needed to complete the project. All of that now has to be obtained somehow.

In some cases, the items may already exist and the WBS will involve only the labor or man-hours to use them—for instance, in a software development project where the goal is to reuse as much of an existing program as possible. In construction-type projects, the reuse of existing equipment may require only relocation labor.

During the "what to procure" phase of the cycle, you will begin the process of breaking the work down into logical packages. Imagine if you would a developer building a small housing project. He could break the work down in one of several ways, and prepare his procurement cycle ac-

Vertical versus horizontal structure

cordingly. For example, he could assign each house to a separate project manager who would be responsible for getting everything done on his house. This would mean that the contractor would arrange for his own framing crew, plumber, electrician, painter, and so on. You could refer to this process as a form of vertical integration. As an alternate, the developer could hire one framing crew to do all of the houses, one plumber to handle all of the plumbing needs, one electrician . . . in a form of horizontal integration. The reasons to choose one over the other might include a lack of large enough firms to handle the entire load, a desire to reduce risk in case one of the firms could not perform, and a sense of competition among the crews. On the other hand, a desire for minimum cost might drive the decision to a larger scale operation with reduced overhead.

Why Contract?

This is the classic make or buy decision. This decision has to be made for every product, either goods or labor, which has to be obtained. This is a management decision and will be based on a number of factors, many of which may not be in harmony with the project goals.

> **Should you make it, or should you buy it?**

Bear in mind that the make or buy decision is not just for the implementation phase of the project. Preliminary engineering for a new facility can be done with in-house resources, or can be contracted out to an engineering company. As a hybrid of this, the engineering company might be used to supply personnel to work in your facility under your direction. Similarly, in a software development project you might well use contract personnel to augment your own staff.

Remember also that "buy" may not be forever. In some case, the contract written will be an "evergreen"—one that runs until some mutually agreeable milestone is met, but may be continued by mutual agreement. This is common with sellers of commodity-type items such as building services or, valves, or other nondifferentiated products.

In another case, the "buy" decision might be to rent something from the outside rather than use existing assets. Many projects will rent a crane rather than use one that the facility already has due to the costs associated with standby if the plant's crane is not available when needed.

Here are some influences on the make or buy decision:

MAKE

Available plant capacity
Workforce is available
May be a proprietary product; secrecy
Avoid using a project manager
Provincialism; nobody can do it like we can
Cheaper
We really might be better
Easier to make changes; no contract to worry about

BUY

Specialists can do the work better
Specialists can do the work cheaper
Buyer lacks technical skills
Buyer lacks time
Buyer lacks design capability
Control over scope
Warranties
Innovation

What Types of Contracts to Use

The selection of what type of contract to use is critical at this stage because this decision will have a major bearing on how detailed the procurement documents must be, the degree of risk you are willing to assume, and the degree of supervision that will be required during the implementation phase. Before I get into the detail of the types of contracts, let me offer some definitions concerning contracts.

▶ *Contract.* A contract is a mutually binding agreement between two or more parties that is enforceable in court. Contracts are characterized by the following five criteria:

- *Offer.* One party who is competent to do so makes an offer to provide a product or service to the other party. This offer is binding unless it is revoked prior to acceptance by the other party, or expires on a date by which the other party must accept the offer.

- *Acceptance.* The other party acknowledges the offer and agrees to accept the product or service. This acceptance may be in writing, verbal, or by the action of using the product or service. The latter can be confusing and should be avoided.

- *Consideration.* Something of value is exchanged for the goods or services offered. While the most common type of consideration is money, there is no requirement that this be the case. Barter contracts exchange goods for goods or services for services for, example.

- *Legal purpose.* Agreements to perform activities or supply goods that are illegal are not contracts in that they are not enforceable in the court system. These sorts of agreements tend to use a more direct form of enforcement, and the verdict is generally not subject to appeal!

- *Competent parties.* Contracts must be entered into by parties that are competent to do so. This does not mean that they are trained, or know what they are doing. In this case competent means authorized. It is also required that the two parties are separate legal entities. While it is common to refer to agreements within a company as "contracts," these agreements do not meet the competent party definition, nor are the parties separate entities. In this case, there exists a single individual in the organization, no matter how high up, that has the authority to cancel the agreement.

▶ *Subcontract.* This is generally thought of as an additional contract that is entered into by a "prime" contractor. It has all of the characteristics of a contract and is generally thought of in terms of buying a piece of the work through someone else. For example, a general contractor hired to build a house might "sub-out" the electrical, heating and air-conditioning, and landscaping. In fact, many builders are know as "vest pocket" contractors because they do not perform any of the work with their own personnel; rather they keep a bunch of subcontracts in their "vest pocket." The term subcontract is also commonly used to describe contracting with another firm to handle some of the routine chores of running a business. Examples would be lawn mowing and janitorial services.

▶ *Buyer.* There are many terms for the entity that is acquiring a product or service: owner, procurer, customer, or a variety of

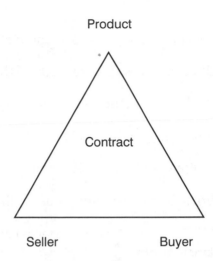

Figure 12.1   Product

other names. For our purposes, the person or firm that is getting

the service or product is the **BUYER.**

▶ *Seller.* Likewise, it is important to have a common term for the

person or organization that is supplying the goods or service. Al-

though they might refer to themselves as vendors, suppliers, or

contractors for our purposes they are **SELLERS.**

▶ *Product.* We will use the term "product" to define that which is

the subject of the contract. This term will substitute for ones

such as goods, services, items, and so on.

There are basically only three types of contracts that you will commonly use:

▶ *Fixed price.* Also referred to as lump sum or hard money con-

tracts, these obligate the seller to provide products at a predeter-

mined price.

▶ *Cost reimbursable.* In this type of contract, the seller will be paid for all of the costs that are incurred, including direct and indirect costs. Some variation of a fee arrangement is also included. Common types are fixed fee and percentage fee.

▶ *Unit rate.* Often used for professional services, this type of contract specifies the rate per unit (hours in the case of professional services) at which the buyer will reimburse the seller. Another common use of this type of contract is the unit rate contact used in construction, where quantities may not be absolutely known.

There are only three basic types of contract

Each of the three types of contract has advantages and disadvantages. The following table outlines some of these for the three basic contracting methods:

Fixed Price

Advantages	Disadvantages
All risk is assumed by the seller	More detailed documents are needed
Less cost for the buyer to manage	Seller may scrimp on quality
Seller has incentive to control cost	Everything is an "extra"
"Total" price is known	Buyer pays for risk whether it happens or not
Commonly used form of contract	Total bid package is needed, taking more time

Cost Reimbursable

Advantages	Disadvantages
Buyer only pays for risks when they occur	Takes more resources from buyer to manage
Can get started earlier	Independent auditing may be needed
Scope can be developed as time passes	Seller has little incentive to control cost
Good when there is a lot of uncertainty	"Scope creep" is common
Changes are easy	Total cost is unknown

Unit Rate

Advantages	Disadvantages
Fixes unit cost before units are known	There is profit and overhead in every unit
Good for professional services	Little control on total cost
There are no change procedures needed	Requires a lot of buyer management
A kind of hybrid fixed fee	Buyers are unfamiliar with this type of contract
Scope is simple and quick	

This does not mean that that penalty should be only a slap on the wrist. Major projects have major cost implications, including direct costs, indirect costs, and opportunity costs.

Another less frequently seen contract variation has to do with an economic price adjustment (EPA). Such contracts are used to protect both parties in a highly inflationary environment. They establish some independent indicator to allow for price changes in selected items if the index rises or falls by a certain amount. This protects both parties in that it removes an element of risk. Were it not for the EPA, a seller might have to inflate his bid to cover the possible increase, but the higher figure might cause him to lose the bid. If the seller were to win the work at the higher price, then the buyer would pay the higher price whether the increase occurred or not.

Teaming arrangements and partnering are two variations in which two or more companies agree to work together on the endeavor. This might be between a buyer and a seller, or it may be the case whereby two sellers jointly bid and manage the work along some defined guidelines.

Project Procurement Plan for Subcontracting

Once the decisions have been finalized as to what needs to be procured, where it will be obtained, and what type of contract will be used for the

> **The procurement plan documents the decisions made during the process**

"buy" items, you will need to develop a procurement plan that outlines how the remainder of the procurement process will be handled. Items to be included in such a plan include, at a minimum:

▶ Statement of work for each task identified for purchase in the make or buy analysis.

▶ What type of contract will be used for each?

▶ Will custom procurement documents be needed, and if so how will they be developed?

▶ Who in the organization will handle what activities, and what can you do independently of the procurement department?

▶ How will the procurement activities be integrated into the budget and schedule? Who will perform these activities?

SOLICITATION PLANNING

Once the basics of the procurement plan have been put into place, the next step is to decide how to go about soliciting bids from the various sellers that might supply the product you require. In this phase you will have to develop a bidder's list and develop the outline for the documents that will be needed to solicit bids. As important, you will need to integrate each solicitation into the project schedule.

The following items need to be considered at this phase:

▶ Sources of seller information

▶ Qualification of sellers

▶ Types of seller selection

▶ Development of the procurement schedule

Sources of Seller Information

In order to select sellers of the product, you will have to develop a vendor list. There are a variety of ways to approach this. How you do so will be determined by a number of factors, such as:

▶ *Existing contracts.* Often the product that is needed is one that is already being used in the business. In this case, the preferred seller might well be the existing vendor. This is especially true when the existing vendor has developed a partnering agreement with the firm. In many cases, there will be provisions for extra work built into the contract, and the project can simply "piggy-back" on the existing agreement.

▶ *Blanket orders.* The blanket order is similar to the existing contract situation. Generally, blanket orders are for commodity-type items such as personal computers or valves and fittings, although they are also found in professional service activities such as programming or design engineering. Typically, the blanket order will have clearly defined limits (motors less than 100 horsepower, for example).

▶ *Vendor technology presentations.* Sellers are particularly interested in making sure that buyers know about their products. However, the typical sales call is not usually effective when it comes time to select vendors. The use of a vendor technology presentation will allow the buyer to gain the needed technical information without the complication of a sales call.

In setting up a vendor technology presentation, make sure that each of the sellers understands that this *will not* be a sales pitch. In fact, it is common to exclude salespeople

❧ ❧
**Vendor
technology
presentations
are not just
glorified
sales calls**
❧ ❧

from the presentation, except perhaps to introduce the technical presenters. Vendors should be given an advance copy of the topics that you would like to discuss and those that you would just as soon forego. Unless the company is totally new to you, items such as annual sales, manufacturing location, and the like are just time-wasters.

You should send the sellers the following information:

■ The nature of the contemplated project. This can be a condensed version of the scope if that is appropriate. Sketches or drawings would help.

■ What capacities you are interested in.

- The timing you anticipate for selecting a vendor. This is needed so that the vendor can anticipate the production impact of any potential order.

- Who will participate from the buyer's side, and what their function on the team will be. Also, let the seller know if non-project team people will be present, and what their interest is.

- Other information that will help them make the presentation useful.

You should ask for the following information:

- The seller's view of the *latest* technology.

- The seller's view of the *appropriate* technology. These two may not be the same.

- Projects similar to the one you are contemplating.

- References if available.

- What they see in what you sent them that doesn't make sense. Often an outsider's view can make yours clearer.

- A discussion of how they control cost, quality, and schedule when they do a project. Remember, technical competence goes beyond the nuts and bolts of generating the product.

You should expect the following:

- A little bit of a sales pitch. Even the most disciplined techie can't resist pushing the company . . . nor should they.

- A reasonable response to your request. Some vendors will shotgun you with their product line, history of the company, and the likes. You should have no qualms about

> **Expect a little bit of a sales pitch**

stopping the presentation and redirecting it to the requested agenda. In this way you can learn a lot about how closely a vendor will pay attention to you in the future.

- References.

- An offer to arrange a site visit, if appropriate.

> **Beware of anti-trust implications when dealing with competitors**

- The vendor will probably ask who his competition is. (He probably already knows!) Politely tell them that they are not in a competition yet, and that you would prefer that they stick to the agenda.

▶ *Industry associates.* Call others in your industry and get their ideas. Watch out for anti-trust implications.

▶ *Other project team members.* In the situation where an existing contract is already in place for a phase of the project, such as engineering, the provider of that service can be used to recommend and evaluate potential sellers of products for subsequent contracts.

▶ *Trade publications.* Every business has trade publications of some sort that have an advertiser's index. Get copies of your industry's, and the contemplated vendor's trade publications, and read the ads to find out who does what you need done. This is particularly valuable when your project is new to your organization.

▶ *Published sources.* Companies such as Sweet's Catalog™ and the Thomas Register™ list practically everything that is made.

Qualification of Sellers

Now that you have developed a list of potential vendors, it is necessary to check and see if they are qualified to work for your company. If you do not do this, you could be in for some surprises later on. This is an exercise jointly done by purchasing, legal, projects, and safety where appropriate, as in construction projects. Typically, the seller will be sent a questionnaire to fill out and submit back to the buyer. Generally, the questions will relate to:

▶ *Financial stability.* How well can they handle the cash outlays that will be needed before they get paid? You should also run a Dun & Bradstreet on the company for verification. Also check for complaints filed with the Better Business Bureau.

▶ *Insurance.* Do they have the right kind and amounts of insurance to meet your needs? This will be in the contract, and having them know it early on will eliminate delays during negotiations.

▶ *Legal action.* Are there any pending legal actions or patent and copyright issues that could impact their ability to perform, or your ability to use the product being supplied?

▶ *Safety statistics.* In construction and manufacturing projects, it is important to know the seller's safety statistics, injury records, and worker's compensation numbers to predict what sort of safety performance you can anticipate on your site. Beyond concern for human suffering, poor safety records are an issue because they are directly linked to the quality of the other project activities, such as schedule and quality.

▶ *Résumés of key personnel.* The experience of key personnel should be reviewed to ensure that the company is competent to perform the work.

▶ *Trade references.* Find out what their other clients think. Remember that you will generally get a pretty sanitized view of things.

Types of Potential Seller Selection

Now that you have decided which sellers you think are qualified from both technical and business aspects, the type of selection process needs to be addressed. In addition to the blanket order and existing contracts mentioned above, there are several other selection processes you should consider.

▶ *Straight bidding.* This occurs when the buyer sends a bid package to a number of selected sellers and requests that they submit proposals. This is the most commonly used method in nongovernmental work.

▶ *Advertising.* Generally used in governmental projects, the buyer advertises for bids in the official newspaper of the area. Any seller who meets the minimum qualifications may obtain the bid documents and submit a proposal. These types of solicitations may be subject to set-asides for sellers of minority classes.

▶ *Plan rooms.* Common in the construction industry, the plans and specifications can be sent to the local plan room (F. W. Dodge being the best known). Any contractor who wishes to can review the plans and submit a proposal. Of course, plans can also be posted with these services on the Internet.

▶ *Negotiated price.* In this situation, you decide to forego a bidding process and rather meet with each of the sellers and arrive at an agreement with one of them. This could be used in a situation where time is of the essence, such as when the potential profit from what will be produced reduces the risk to a low level.

▶ *Single source.* In a single source, you decide that only one seller can meet the needs or is preferred for some other reason. Company policies generally require documentation of the justification in the purchasing file for auditing purposes.

▶ *Sole source.* This is when there is only one source of the product needed. While a pre qualification might be a formality, it should still be done to provide a "comfort factor."

Solicitation Document Planning

Before the bid documents can be assembled, thought must be given to the specifications that will be included. A lot will depend on the type of contract decided upon in the procurement planning phase.

Specification Completeness

If the decision was to go with fixed fee, then the specifications and drawings must be very detailed and as close to complete as practical. Ninety percent is often thought of as "complete."

> **Specification type and completeness depend on the type of contract**

The remainder will be completed as the project ensues but should not be of sufficient magnitude to impact the seller's bid. If they do, then a change order is appropriate.

A cost reimbursable contract, on the other hand, may be let early in the design phase so that progress can be made even while major decisions have yet to be made. In this case, the specifications are needed when the particular part of the project that they affect is released. Of course, specifications that impact all phases are needed immediately.

Specification Types

In addition to the timing issue is the type of specification that will be used. Generally, there are two broad classes of specifications to be considered:

- ▶ Detailed specifications
- ▶ Performance specifications

Detailed Specifications

Detailed specifications dictate precisely how the product is to be built. They leave little or no latitude with the seller to best engineer the product. Often, these types of specifications are used to make the new product compatible with existing technology. They are also used when the buyer is aware that there are a variety of commercially available solutions but she wants a particular one. An example of this might be the type of roofing for a building. Some of the advantages of detailed specifications are:

- ▶ You know what you want and can use detailed specifications to ensure that the product is made exactly as desired
- ▶ Shop inspections and reviews can be done more readily, since you are familiar with what you should be seeing
- ▶ The seller can begin work immediately, since he will not have to do a lot of development work

▶ You have less concern about the quality of the design capability of the seller

Detailed specifications have disadvantages also. Some of these are:

▶ Not taking advantage of the seller's design expertise

▶ As long as the seller follows the specifications, you have little recourse when "your" design does not perform

▶ They also are more costly for you to prepare and can delay getting the project started

Performance Specifications

Performance specifications are becoming more popular as buyer's staffs become smaller, and the state of the technology involved becomes more complex. These types of specifications concentrate on the ability of the product to *perform* as needed. Some advantages of performance specifications are:

▶ They are often less costly and quicker to prepare than detailed specifications

▶ You can concentrate on what you want done, not how it will be done

▶ The seller probably knows more about the product than you do, as you might do this type of project infrequently

Performance specifications have disadvantages as well. Some of these are:

▶ You do not always fully understand what is going to be delivered

▶ Inspection is more difficult

▶ The details of the design are not known until it is delivered

▶ The design might not fit in with the rest of the project

▶ Procurement time might be longer

Often specifications will be a hybrid of these two. You might provide "plant or company standards" for the seller to follow for common or commodity items. The seller might offer to let you choose between several suppliers for specialty components. There is inherent in this approach the danger that by involving yourself deeply in a "performance" specification type of arrangement you may unwittingly assume responsibility when things go awry. This is not to say that a cooperative agreement cannot be of value. It is important, however, to choose the right contracts for this approach.

One method of contracting for large industrial facilities that depends almost exclusively on performance specifications is the engineer, procure, and construct (EPC) type of contract. In this situation, the seller has a lot of latitude to design the facility using "commercially acceptable" components as long as the final product performs as per the contract. You might choose this type of contract when you have little or no technical expertise or staff. In its purest form, it is a classic example of not knowing what you ordered until it arrives. Generally, however, you will assign one or more representatives to follow the project. Their role would be to answer questions, provide guidance on the selection of materials and equipment, and smooth the integration of the new into the existing.

A variation of this method is the "vendor lead" project. In this form, the seller of the major components is contracted with to supply the design and construction of the entire project, following your performance specification. This type of arrangement can be risky, as the seller of the major equipment may have no expertise in the other areas for which he is made responsible.

STANDARDS

Specifications should not be confused with standards. Standards consist of detailed information developed by official organizations such as the federal government, the American National Standards Institute (ANSI), the International Organization for Standardization (ISO), and any number of trade groups. Standards dictate the minimum requirements to which a product must conform in order to be usable and safe. Standards are generally referenced in specifications. Be careful to have the current version in the reference. Statements such as "Seller shall comply with all applicable standards" may warm the cockles of a lawyer's heart, but they don't do much to make you and the seller understand each other.

There are two broad categories of standards. The first involves regulatory and mandatory standards such as the Occupational Safety and Health Administration (OSHA) and the National Electric Code (NEC). These must be followed on all projects where applicable. The second category is voluntary standards. These are generally developed by trade groups and the like, and are recommended practices. For example, there are standards for floppy disks and copy paper, but you don't have to follow them. As a buyer, you can use off brands if you like. As a seller, however, you must comply if you claim you do.

Another set of standards that should be closely studied is industry or seller's standards. Over the years, industry standards, or conventions, have been developed. Most, if not all, sellers in a particular segment use them for their "stock" products. *Using industry standards is generally the most cost effective way to procure products; you should try to buy what is sold.* Customizing just for the sake of it is expensive, and may unnecessarily add to the schedule.

Finally, there are de facto standards. These have no legal basis, but everyone has adopted them. Computer operating systems are an example. So is the use of critical path method scheduling.

SOLICITATION PROCESS

Now that the decisions have been made regarding what to procure, what type of contract to use, which sellers to solicit, and the technical requirements to include, the next step is to solicit proposals and manage the bidding process

> **It is unethical to obtain a bid from a vendor you would not use**

Please remember that it is unethical and downright wrong to obtain a bid from a vendor you would not use. This is sometimes done to "broaden the field" when there is one favorite seller, but the buyer does not want that seller to know they are favored. Not only do bids cost money to prepare, the bidders are wise to this practice, and you will wind up looking foolish at best.

This section deals with the following topics:

▶ Forms of solicitation

▶ What to include in the solicitation

▶ Activities that should occur during the bidding phase

Forms of Solicitation

There are several terms that can be used for the solicitation that you send to a seller in order to get a price for doing the work outlined. I include them here to assist you in understanding the differences that may be implied by each. There are no hard and fast rules regarding the use of a particular term, and in fact they are frequently used interchangeably even within a given organization. Nonetheless, the terms may cause the seller to draw different inferences.

The most commonly used names for the three primary types of solicitation document are:

▶ Request for proposal (RFP)

▶ Request for quotation (RFQ)

▶ Invitation to bid (IFB)

> **General rule:**
> **RFP suggests cost reimbursable**
> **RFQ suggests unit rate**
> **IFB suggests fixed price**

Request for Proposal

This term is commonly used when you want the seller to develop a solution for a problem, as opposed to simply supplying products that meet the specification.

RFPs are typically used when there is an "intellectual" element to the work. Examples might be conceptual engineering services, performance requirements development, or process-design type activities. In these cases, you depend on the seller to be an extension of your thought process. It is very common for you and seller to work collaboratively.

RFPs are most often thought of for cost reimbursable contracts

Request for Quotation

In this case you know what you want but require an outside source to provide it. You are not looking for advice, but still need the services of the seller. The seller is expected to use appropriate judgment, but not necessarily be innovative.

This form of solicitation might be used for obtaining detailed engineering services, coding activities not involving high-level design, or other "by the hour" type of activities. It also could be used to obtain pricing for multiple future purchases of commodity-type items.

RFQs are frequently thought of when dealing with time and material or unit rate contracts.

Invitation to Bid

In the case where you have a detailed design and specifications, and simply want someone to provide the service, the IFB is appropriate. It simply asks for a price, and defines all of the attributes of the item. Purchasing standard motors would be an example of an IFB, as would be constructing a building that has been completely engineered. Off-the-shelf software items would be another example.

IFBs are most commonly thought of in terms of fixed-price contracts.

Bear in mind that these are generally accepted relationships, not hard and fast rules. Many organizations use the terms interchangeably.

Other Forms of Solicitation

There are times when a form of solicitation might be used other than for the express purpose of obtaining a product from a seller. Sometimes you are not quite ready to commit, but still need the knowledge that the seller has to complete an estimate, for example. In these cases, the following could be used.

Request for Budget Quotation   When preparing an estimate, you can rely on a variety of sources for cost information: previous projects, published databases, rationalization of work hours, and existing contracts, for example. However, there are times that you need outside input.

The request for budget quotation is sent to a seller to get a "budget quote." Generally, all of the documents that would be needed for a formal

RFQ are not in place, and the specific details of the design are far from complete. The seller is, therefore, being asked to guess what details have been omitted. As can be imagined, the price quoted will be attended by caveats that it is preliminary, and that the seller retains the right to refuse to sell at that price.

The price will almost certainly be high. By not including all of the particulars, you have put all of the risk on the seller. It is common to include the budget quote in the final estimate, knowing full well that at the time of purchase a lower price will be negotiated. This "hidden contingency" reflects the realization that the labor component of the project frequently overruns. Kind of a "what you save in the office will be spent in the field" mentality, which has proven to be true much of the time!

Competitive Scoping   A novel approach to the issue of getting the best scope for a project given that the sellers in the industry have similar equipment, but different approaches to its implementation and varying degrees of technical expertise, is the use of competitive scoping.

> **Competitive scoping and reverse auction bidding are two innovative means of procurement**

Competitive scoping works best with strong performance specifications. The goods being obtained from the seller will be used to produce your finished product. As an example, there might be any number of ways to produce charcoal briquettes. You are interested in the cost and quality of the finished briquettes, but have no particular favorite way to produce them, or lack the resources to research all of the options or designs.

Competitive scoping involves soliciting several sellers to design a process to produce low-cost, high-quality charcoal briquettes at an acceptable production rate. All of these requirements would be spelled out in detail in the performance specifications, and a performance guarantee would be solicited as well. The sellers would design and specify a process and the equipment needed to comply with the specifications.

Competitive scoping is expensive for the seller. He has to do a great deal of design work and engineering to develop a viable proposal. In order to encourage sellers to participate in the process, you would agree to pay the actual cost plus an acceptable markup of the unsuccessful bidders. The successful bidder is rewarded with the contract to complete the design and furnish the process and equipment.

Reverse Auction Bidding

The Internet has allowed for the practical use of an innovative form of solicitation called reverse auction bidding. Reverse auction bidding works like this: you, as a buyer, post your requirements with one of several firms that manage reverse auction bidding on the Internet. Sellers post their bids for the work or product at this site. You, as the buyer, can see all of the bids and the companies that are bidding: the sellers can see all of the bids but not the companies against whom they are competing. All of this occurs in real time, and it may take only a few minutes or hours.

Reverse auction bidding was originally developed to purchase commodity items such as plastic pellets or chemicals. It is now being used for more complicated purchases. As you might imagine, strong opinions about the use of the procedure exist.

What to Include in the Solicitation

In most nongovernment projects, there is no standard format for soliciting a proposal. Indeed, the forms of solicitation can even vary within a given organization, depending on the circumstances. In general, however, there are certain items that should be included regardless of the contract type or project circumstances. These are included to inform all parties as to the particulars of the contract and to eliminate confusion and unnecessary claims in the future. Note the word "unnecessary." There are necessary claims, and the change management section of contract administration will handle these.

At a minimum, the solicitation should include the following sections:

▶ Introduction and instructions to bidder

▶ Scope of work (SOW)

▶ Form of proposal

▶ Drawings and specifications

▶ Special conditions

▶ General conditions and proposed form of contract

Details of these sections follow.

Introduction and Instructions to Bidders

The introduction and instructions to bidders outlines for the bidders what will be needed to satisfy the buyer's request for a proposal. It outlines specific details pertinent to the bid and serves as an invitation to sellers to submit their bids. Some of the items covered could be:

A general description of the work. Not to be confused with the scope of work (SOW), the general description of the work outlines in summary what the bidder is being asked to do, when the work will be accomplished, and how you will interact with the seller during the purchase.

Schedule of bidding activities. This section specifies the date the bids are due. Most solicitations have strict rules concerning when bids are due and what should be done in the event that the date cannot be met. If a bidder notifies you that the bid date cannot be met, you can either extend the bidding period for all bidders or inform the late bidder that the date is

Tell the bidders what they need to know

firm. It is unfair to the competent bidders to do otherwise. The location and means of bid submittal will also be specified. If you will accept fax copies of the bid, this should also be noted. Most public entities require public bid openings. Most private ones do not.

This section can also identify contacts in your organization for questions during the process. Note that typically there are two types of questions, technical and commercial. Most companies insist that commercial questions be directed to the purchasing agent. Technical questions are frequently asked of the project team. There is an inherent risk in this scenario. While answering a technical question you may inadvertently impact the commercial aspects of the bid. This is due to the fact that the seller might raise an issue that you had not thought of and that might subsequently cause that seller to include extras in the bid that the others do not. This puts the first seller at an economic disadvantage and confuses the entire process. A preferred way to handle questions is to hold a pre-bid conference, or at least require all questions of any nature to go to the purchasing agent, who will then get responses from others. While this may stifle a creative dialog, it keeps the playing field level.

The schedule of bidding activities section should also specify the starting date of the contract, as well as is known at the time. Bidders may decide that this timing does not fit their work schedule and thus "no-bid" the work and save the cost of preparing a bid they cannot honor. Any required meetings or visits should be mentioned here as well.

Location of the work. For contracts that involve work at your site, bidders need to be told where the work will be performed. This is also valuable for service-type contracts, as bidders will need to know what infrastructure is available to support their personnel. This would include travel and living arrangements, and second-tier support such as electronic stores or building supplies. The location will also impact the price in terms of shipping, travel, and the like.

Evaluation criteria. It can be of value for you to tell the bidders how you intend to evaluate the proposals. This is not to say that you should send detailed evaluation criteria to the bidders, but if schedule is an overriding consideration bidders need to know this, as a rush job will cost more. Similarly, if you want the best technical solution, with cost and schedule being secondary, this should be made known to the bidders as well, since it will impact the personnel that might be assigned.

Type of contract required. You need to tell the seller what type of contract will be used. You also should explain any incentives that will be used. This is critical, because the type of contract has direct implications as to whether you or the seller is going to assume the risk.

Policies during bidding. You should tell bidders what sorts of activities are

> **Tell the bidders to let you know if they are going to bid**

inappropriate during the bidding period. Gifts and entertainment should be prohibited, as these will certainly taint the ethical nature of the bidding process. There are better times to hand out coffee mugs and ball caps!

Letter of acknowledgment and intent to bid. The instructions should include a form letter to be filled out and returned acknowledging receipt of the solicitation and specifying whether or not a bid will be submitted. It is remarkable how many times a seller will no-bid a solicitation. If one or more bidders drop out, you need the time to select alternate bidders to keep the process competitive. You also may want to reevaluate what you are asking for, as a couple of no-bids should raise a red flag concerning the details of the project.

Most commonly, the no-bidders do not have the resources to adequately handle the job if they were to get it. However, many companies have policies regarding certain types of contracts and refuse to bid on them. It is common for engineering firms to no-bid fixed fee work on conceptual engineering.

Scope of Work (SOW)

The scope of work (SOW) must be included to ensure that bidders understand what is being asked of them. For simple contracts, a simple scope of work is all that is needed. In many cases, in fact, a special type of contract, referred to as a purchase order, is all that is required for most routine purchases. More complex projects, however, require a great deal of detail to ensure that bidders know what is in the package, and specifically what is excluded from the package. This prevents bidders from making assumptions about the work. Being cute about trying to hide requirements from the bidders will not only foul up this project, but a lot of no-bids will occur in the future.

Special site requirements can be handled here or in the special conditions. While not common in many service contracts or intellectual endeavors, virtually all construction contracts require the seller to provide separate entrances, especially in the case of an open shop, or non-union, contractor in a union company. Sellers also have to provide their own sanitary facilities and office spaces.

Of particular importance is your intent to go beyond the bare minimum in certain regulatory standards. If you have a more stringent safety or environmental policy, you should spell it out here, or in the general conditions section.

Form of Proposal

In order for a bidder to adequately comply with the commercial section of the solicitation, you have to tell him what is expected. The form of proposal should be included in

> **Tell the bidders what you expect from them**

an outline form that requires the bidder to fill out all sections. This ensures that all bidders are bidding on the same thing.

Some typical requirements in a form of proposal are:

Bid price. The dollar amount at which the seller will provide the products specified, subject to the terms and conditions in the solicitation. In the case of a reimbursable contract, the price may be a good faith estimate or a "not to exceed," since a firm price cannot be determined.

Bid price breakdown. It is desirable that you get a breakdown of the bid price so that you can compare it to the estimate and use the information for cost control. Giving the bidders a copy of the work breakdown structure (WBS) that was used to develop the estimate can do this. You could also send a copy of the estimate format with quantities and dollars removed so that the bidder can fill in the blanks with his information. This would help structure the bid in a way that would be easy to compare to the original thinking.

In a reimbursable contract, bidders should provide the labor cost per hour, the cost basis for supplying materials and equipment, any warehousing charges for handling buyer-supplied equipment, and a "multiplier" for indirect costs. This multiplier is an add on to each direct labor hour, and covers such things as profit and overhead and costs required by statute, such as FICA (Social Security), unemployment insurance (FUI and SUI), and worker's compensation.

In a fixed-fee environment, however, the price breakdown is difficult to get with any accuracy, and what is delivered will frequently be of little value. There are several reasons for this that the buyer should understand:

► Bidders, quite properly, do not think that how they arrived at their price is any of your business. If you want to see the cost structure, you must accept the bid and issue a contract to get it.

► Bidders are afraid that you might "shop the bid." This is a process whereby you let the other bidders know how much they need to come down to meet the competition. If the bidders supply a breakdown of the bid, you can use sections where the bidder is low to influence the other bidders. This is a highly unethical practice. It also jeopardizes the working relationships on a project and almost always leads to substandard quality.

► The bidder may have "front loaded" the job. Since the progress payment terms will specify how much cash is released against a particular portion of work, it is in the bidder's best interest in the short term to get as much money up front as possible. By not pro-

Not all proposals are scientific

viding a cost breakdown, the bidder can get this set up on a time basis, in the form of monthly payments. As an example, if a seller is installing a network, and can get paid 30 percent for running the conduit instead of the 10 percent that you had in mind, the seller does not want the buyer to have details of his cost.

Similarly, installing 100 feet of driveway entails excavation before the paving work can begin. If the bidder had this in at 5 percent, but could get paid 10 percent when it is finished, he would be ahead. While this may seem devious, bear in mind that most contracts provide for withholding "retainage" to the tune of 10 percent on the entire contract. This is almost always more than the seller's profit. In a sense, the buyer has the seller financing the job.

▶ Lastly, the bidder may not have a good basis for supplying the information. Contrary to what many may think, the process of deciding what to bid is generally pretty unscientific. Of course, there is structure in doing material takeoffs and applying labor to the job, but decisions on profit and overhead are far more subjective. They depend greatly on the state of the bidder's workload and how "hungry" they are. It is amazing how many bids are decided moments before they are submitted. This is why you often see a handwritten price in an otherwise typed proposal.

Extra Work Provisions

The time to get the bidders to agree on the provisions for extra work is before the contract is let. If the contract is let without these being specified, the seller has little incentive to offer a good price.

> **Get time and material rates *before* signing a contract**

Of course, in any form of reimbursable or unit rate environment this is already known.

If these provisions are established, then any extra work can be done on a time and materials basis, freeing you from requesting firm prices and issuing new contracts or change orders. You must always reserve the right to request a firm price for extra work. However, if the scope is ill defined, the T&M method is probably better.

Schedule Provisions

The bidder should be asked to commit to a schedule for the work during the bidding process. Assuming that the work commences within a specified time frame, the schedule will become part of the contract.

Key Personnel

Bidders should be required to provide the names of key personnel that will be on the job and commit to leave them there until you release them. This is critical, because the key person often will be the deciding factor in your decision. This is especially true in the case of intellectual work or conceptual engineering.

Subcontractors

A listing of proposed subcontractors and suppliers needs to be submitted with the bid so that you can be comfortable with who is going to do the work.

You can also specify what parts of the work may be subcontracted, and what may not. This is to prevent the seller from subcontracting the whole job and running it in name only.

Solicitation Documents Used in the Bid

As covered later, you must supply a set of documents with an index showing the revision number of each. During the bidding process, however, revisions may be sent out. The bidders must supply a list of documents upon which they have based their bid, and conflicts need to be resolved.

Errors and Clarifications

You should direct bidders to immediately notify the buyer of bid document discrepancies. You, through purchasing, should notify all bidders of the resolution in writing as an addendum.

Clarifications and Exceptions

The bidder needs to notify you of any clarifications that were made by the bidder to the RFP and also any exceptions that are being taken. It is a rare set of RFP documents that is crystal clear. For example, the RFP may not include subsurface investigation information for a building. The bidder should take exception, and clarify that the bid is based on suitable conditions and any variation will cause an extra work order. Very few contractors stay in business if they miss these sorts of things.

Duration of Validity of the Bid

The bidder should state for how long he will honor the bid. This is only fair, in that he has assets potentially committed and cannot seek other work until this bid is resolved.

Signature of an Officer

The bid must have the signature of an officer of the company and include any license requirements you or the government has imposed.

Drawings and Specifications

There needs to be a complete set of drawings and specifications submitted with the solicitation so that the bidders will know exactly what to price. The index must specify the revision number that is being issued. This is true for all types of contracts, even though the true cost-plus type could be bid without them, since you are going to pay for everything anyway and the seller is simply providing labor and materials as directed. However, if the bidder does not have the needed documents to ensure that he is willing and competent to provide the product if awarded, then a trap has been set that will hurt both sides.

In some instances, the drawings and specifications may contain work not in the scope of the solicitation. It may be that the documents are part of a larger project and this solicitation is for only a part. This is common in the contracting method referred to as "multiple lump sums," where you are providing project management services for a number of independent fixed-fee contracts. In this case, the drawings and specifications need to be clearly marked to identify the work.

Drawings and specifications need to be referenced in the scope of work, and will become part of the contract documents.

Special Conditions

A critical topic to be covered in special conditions has to do with how the project will be managed, and what efforts will be required of the seller to comply with these needs. The special conditions should outline progress-reporting requirements, cost information to be delivered to you, meeting schedules and places, and site conditions that are out of the ordinary.

These and other conditions are important because they all have costs associated with them and may impact the work done at the site. Imagine what would happen if the seller was not told that the progress meetings were to be held in Hong Kong!

Special site conditions may include the need for escorts for non-U.S. citizens, interpreters, extreme security measures, and safety requirements that are not the norm.

General Conditions and Proposed Form of Contract

This is the section where you spell out for the seller the commercial aspects of the job. Included here would be change provisions, payment information, legal responsibilities, nonperformance remedies, and similar items. A copy of the proposed contract should also be included, so the bidder can understand what will be expected of him should he get the award.

As is often the case, the legal and purchasing groups develop this section of the solicitation. They generally reuse previous contracts, and over time these become so burdened with conditions that they become difficult to understand by those outside of these specialties. You need to work with these two groups to fully comprehend what the bidder is being asked to do and what his team's responsibilities are.

Bidders will almost certainly take exception to some contract terms and conditions. This will be noted in their bid, and the differences will have to be negotiated.

Activities during the Bidding Phase

There exists a time between when the solicitation is issued and the date that the bids are due that can be a very productive and busy time. This is when you will manage the process to ensure that the bids are complete and competent. Several activities need to be underway during this time, and a number of things may arise that should alert you to potential problems.

Pre-Bid Conference

In order to get competent bids, you should require a pre-bid conference. This is an ideal

> **Every seller should attend the pre-bid meeting at the same time**

opportunity for potential bidders and your project team to get together and ensure that the solicitation was clear as to what the bidders are being asked to provide. The alternative—sitting back and waiting for bidders to call—may result in no calls, and therefore a false sense of completeness in the documents. The other danger is that you may answer the various bidders differently at different times. This can only lead to confusion, and therefore poor-quality, incomplete bids.

Not all RFPs require a pre-bid conference, however. Typically they are not needed for shelf items, and they should be carefully considered for small-dollar projects where the cost of attending might not be warranted. Essentially, all engineering or development contracts should have a pre-bid. Construction contracts must have them.

The elements of a pre-bid conference are essentially the same as any other well-run project meeting. The purpose is to gain and give information. Some of these elements are:

Purpose. The purpose of the pre-bid meeting is to ensure that all bidders received the complete package, and that the RFP was sufficiently clear to allow all bidders to develop a complete and competent bid. At this meeting you can emphasize the areas of the RFP that are of particular importance. For example, if schedule is of overriding importance, the bidders should be reminded of this.

In addition to your being able to fully explain the RFP, the pre-bid meeting allows for further assessment of the bidder's technical and commercial ability and interest in the project, and also provides feedback as to the quality of the solicitation package. Ambiguous language in the solicitation should elicit questions from bidders that have fully studied the document.

Agenda. The agenda for the meeting should include a discussion of the scope of work and a review of the documents. Following this overview, you should cover your expectations regarding the technical aspects of the project, the schedule requirements, and the quality standards that were in the package. This should be a review of what was sent out, not new information for the bidders! The purchasing manager should discuss the commercial requirements. If the contract involves sharing of cost data, such as in a reimbursable contract, the cost accounting representative should ensure that bidders understand the scope and timing of the presentation of this information during the project.

Who should attend? You, your project team, and the purchasing/contracts department should attend the meeting. The group should decide in advance how the meeting is to be conducted, and should follow the published agenda, which should be sent to all bidders prior to the meeting. In many cases, the agenda could be included in the solicitation documents. Typically, you would begin the meeting, and turn it over to specialists as appropriate. In most organizations, the purchasing manager would be the only one to discuss commercial terms. This is to keep the rest of the team focused on the technical details. Also, in most organizations, only the purchasing department can make financial commitments for the firm.

All bidders must attend at the same time. It is critical that every bidder hears the same explanations and questions. Bidders should be required to send the proposed project manager unless it would require extraordinary effort to do so, such as when the person is on another critical job. You would not want the person pulled off of your job to go to a meeting with another client. In extreme circumstances, the use of video conferencing should be considered.

You should be very leery of a bidder who sends only a salesman to the pre-bid meeting. This lack of commitment to the project can only spell disaster in the future. Having the project manager present allows you to assess his technical competence and also get a reading on how the two teams will relate to one another. Compatible personalities and style can certainly help a project, particularly when conflicts arise.

When and where should the meeting be held? Don't schedule the meeting so close to the issuing of the documents that the bidders have insufficient time to understand what is being asked of them. The more complex the project, the longer bidders will need to digest the material. On a fast-track project, this delay can be frustrating, but a failure to do the pre-bid meeting right will cost you in the long run, especially on a fixed-fee contract where every change generates an extra.

The location of the meeting depends on the type of project that is being bid. Your site may be the best option, but often on engineered projects the office of the design engineer is better. This is because the engineer will

When and where should the meeting take place?

have available the technical personnel that worked on the design, and is therefore in a better position to address questions and concerns. It is costly to have a large contingent from the engineer travel to your site.

If the work is to be done at the site, or if viewing the site would make the bidders better informed, then the site should be the location.

Questions and answers. Bidders' questions should be answered at the meeting. In addition, they should be documented in writing and sent to all bidders in the form of an addendum to the solicitation, along with any other clarifications that arise during the meeting. Bidders that do not attend the pre-bid meeting should also get the addendum.

Questions before and after the pre-bid meeting are generally handled differently. The initiative of one bidder to improve his bid by asking further questions outside of the pre-bid meeting should not be "rewarded" by giving the information to his competitor. However, questions asked outside of the pre-bid meeting that uncover a serious flaw in the documents should be addressed to all involved. In extreme cases, the solicitation may be withdrawn for rework.

It is a good policy to have the procurement department be the only one to receive questions, to ensure consistency in the answers given to the bidders. It can be time consuming and somewhat cumbersome to follow this policy, but having bidders calling different members of the project team can lead to conflicting answers, and in some cases the project team member may give information that is contrary to the contractual terms being presented.

Site Visits

At the conclusion of the pre-bid meeting, bidders should be escorted on a site visit, if the type of project warrants one. There is certainly no harm in a site visit for all projects where the pre-bid is held at the buyer's location, but projects that are to be done solely at the bidder's facility probably would not gain anything from a site visit.

Construction or installation contracts should have formal site visits set up in addition to the pre-bid meeting. The site visits should be held after the pre-bid, so that the personnel visiting the site have the advantage of the explanations given and the questions asked and answered.

The reason for a separate site visit is that the bidder's staff that attend the pre-bid meeting will generally not include everyone that needs to see the

> ❧ ❧
>
> **The bidders should be escorted on a site visit, if the type of project warrants one**
>
> ❧ ❧

site. For example, on a large or complex project, the size of the staff that should attend the site visit would make the pre-bid meeting too large and unwieldy. Also, many of the items that are discussed in the site visit may not be discussed in the pre-bid. For that reason, the same rules and guidelines that were developed for the pre-bid apply as well to a site visit. Finally, the pre-bid may not always be held at the site (such as when it is held at the buyer's engineers' facility).

Site visits as described above are so critical that they should be made a condition of the bid. If a bidder cannot make the site visit at the time arranged, an alternate date can be set up to accommodate them. However, this is not desirable for the same reason the separate pre-bid meetings are a bad idea. The logistics of a site visit sometimes warrant bending this rule, especially if the bidder that needs it is particularly well qualified.

Bidder's site visits.   There is a benefit to visiting the bidder's site during the bidding period. Often, the bidder has not been able to assemble his entire proposed project team by the time of the pre-bid. The information gained in the pre-bid will allow him to select the appropriate team members. Also, previous visits to the bidder's office would not be as fruitful since the bidder did not have the details of the project under consideration. All bidders should be visited if any are to be visited, to avoid the appearance of favoritism. The visits should concentrate on the qualifications of the bidders, and not be an extension of the pre-bid meeting. However, once again, information that reveals a significant flaw in the solicitation should be shared with all bidders.

Visiting the bidder can also provide insight into the bidder's workload. This can be valuable during contract negotiations. Empty offices and nonproducing machinery are expensive.

Other Considerations during the Bidding Period

There are other things to think about during the bidding period. The results of the pre-bid meeting and the site visits may reveal items to be taken care of regardless of which bidder proves successful. Perhaps there is a need to clear out a work area for the seller once the project begins. Maybe the drawings and specifications need to be made clearer and be reissued. It is possible that another project will have to be rearranged so as to allow both to proceed. If you need to hire contract staff or an outside auditor to monitor the seller's performance, this may be the time to do it.

If the evaluation criteria have not been developed, they should be before the bids are reviewed. Once the bids are studied, the development of objective criteria becomes more difficult.

What to Avoid during the Bidding Period

Just as there are certain things that must be done during the bidding period, there are those that must not be done. The following actions can tarnish the process:

Socializing with bidders. It is almost certain that one or more of the bidders will offer to take the team to dinner or some sort of sporting event during the bidding period. Do not allow this to happen. One way to head this off is to declare a no-socializing policy in the pre-bid meetings and site visits. It is

> **Your reputation is worth more than a ballpoint pen!**

fairly common for the buyer to provide lunch during the pre-bid meetings, or perhaps host a dinner afterward. Bidders should not be allowed to do so.

Accepting gifts from the bidders. The time to accept coffee cups and baseball caps is during a sales call, when there is no project under consideration. Most companies have policies along this line, and this policy should be reviewed with the bidders at the pre-bid meeting. Your reputation for integrity is worth more than a ballpoint pen!

Sharing bidder's innovations. Some of the questions that are received outside of the pre-bid and site visits might reveal that one bidder has developed an innovation that can save significant time or money during the project. This innovation should not be shared with the other bidders. It should be reserved as a competitive advantage for the bidder who originated it. In the circumstance that this bidder is *not* the successful one, the innovation can be discussed with the bidder that did get the job. In the case of a reimbursable contract, the savings will accrue automatically. In a fixed-fee arrangement, the buyer and seller would have to negotiate the savings.

Sharing bidder's cost information. From time to time, a bidder will reveal some of his cost figures to you. The purpose of this is generally to make sure he is on the right track and has not seriously under- or overestimated the scope of work. That cost information is his business, and it is unfair to share it with others. This kind of information must never be solicited outside of the bidding process.

SOURCE SELECTION

The solicitation process ends when you receive the bids. As mentioned earlier, this must be a formal process whereby all bidders will have their complete bid package to your purchasing representative no later than a predetermined time. (Bidders can certainly send bids in early.)

Bids should not be opened until the time stated in the solicitation. This is true even when there is not a public opening, as in government contracts. This is because the bid should be subject to revision until the time specified. If a bidder sends his in early and then discovers a mistake, he should be allowed to rework the bid. For purposes of the discussion of source selection, we will assume that all bidders met the time and did not have to recall their bids. We will also assume that there are no gross material errors that could lead to the bidder refusing to take the work and the subsequent legal activities that may occur

Source selection involves evaluating the bids from technical, management, and commercial aspects. This requires the development of criteria by which the bids can be judged for compliance with the solicitation. Generally, this step would be followed by a series of post-bid reviews for further exploring the bids. At this step the decision will be made concerning which bidders will continue in the selection process.

Following the evaluation, you will make your recommendation. Once approved by management, final negotiations will follow, with the goal of a contract award.

Evaluation Criteria

To adequately and fairly evaluate the proposals that are received, you must develop a set of evaluation criteria. These should be developed before the proposals are opened so that the criteria and weighting can be done objectively, and not with prejudice toward a particular seller. This prejudice is unavoidable once the proposals are reviewed.

Different types of solicitations lead to different types of evaluations. The simplest is for commodity or shelf items that are made to industry standards and for which a simple invitation to bid (IFB) was issued. As an example, if the IFB was for tape dispensers and a part number was called out in the IFB, the evaluation form would look like this:

$$\boxed{\textbf{PRICE: 100\%}}$$

Obviously, you would not be involved in evaluating such a bid, but someone must do the evaluation. There will be further discussion on the particulars of the evaluation criteria in subsequent sections.

Evaluation Criteria Format Development

In order to carry out the technical, managerial, and commercial evaluation, it is helpful to use a standard format. This is beneficial because each team member will do the evaluation using the exact same criteria that the others on the team are using. Bear in mind, however, that the criteria must be developed

> **Develop evaluation criteria and techniques before looking at the bids**

separately for each of the technical, managerial, and commercial evaluations, and not all team members will be needed on each type of evaluation.

The development of the evaluation criteria should follow a format of identifying and quantifying items that are important to you. For example, if you have a very inexperienced technical staff, then the bidder's expertise will be one of the criteria to be evaluated. Conversely, if the company already runs a receiving warehouse, the bidder's abilities in this area would be far less important.

Be cautious about the number of criteria that you include on the list. Ten would probably be a maximum. Too many makes the analysis difficult to handle. If there is a need for in-depth review of a particular item, such as the proposed scheduling system on a complex job, you could make up a separate worksheet and identify the pertinent items for the scheduling analysis. This could be forwarded to the managerial summary if necessary.

Once the criteria have been established and a consensus reached among your project team, you should decide on the relative weighting that each of the items should receive. This is typically done so that the total weighting equals 100 points. Other ways could be used, but by capping the total at 100 you are forced to make tradeoffs, since it is unlikely that all of the criteria are of equal importance.

How to spread the 100 points depends on the type of project the proposal addresses. One that supplies a single item would likely be spread differently from one that supplies custom computer software. Remember that the exercise is to emphasize those items that are critical to the selection decision. Therefore, the smaller weighting should probably be 5 percent, or even higher. If an item doesn't impact 5 percent of the decision, it might just as well be taken off the list.

The last step in designing the evaluation matrix is to establish a ranking system for each of the criteria. Typically this involves a 1-to-5 or 1-to-10 scale. Don't get overly scientific about this whole exercise. The purpose is to provide guidelines for making what is essentially a subjective exercise a little more objective. It is also designed to get beyond the fancy binders and pictures. Remember that the *weight* of the proposal is not a good indicator of the *quality* of the proposal!

In the ranking of 1-to-5, 1 would be the lowest score, meaning the proposal was poor on that element; 5 would mean that the bidder would be exceptional in that particular aspect of the job.

Therefore, our evaluation criteria form might look something like this:

Seller's Name					
Evaluation Factor	Weight (% of Total)	Times	Score (1–5)	Equals	Weighted Score
1		×		=	
2		×		=	
3		×		=	
4		×		=	
5		×		=	
6		×		=	
Total	100%				

Who Should Do the Evaluation?

The question of who does the evaluation must be addressed. One recommendation is to keep the technical and management system evaluation separate from the commercial evaluation, even to the extent of having the proposals sent in two different forms. The unpriced copy would go to the project team members who are to do the technical and managerial evaluations and would not contain the commercial section, nor would it contain the amount of the bid. The procurement department would receive a priced copy that contains the entire proposal.

The evaluation on the technical and managerial aspects of the job might involve different team members, depending on the type of project. For instance, the technical evaluation might include the engineering or technical staff, the operations or user representative, and the maintenance or systems people. When the managerial criteria are evaluated, the controller or accounting department and the procurement or contracts group should be involved.

After the technical and managerial evaluations have been completed, you and other staff, as needed, should rank the bidders in order of preference. It is often the case in these evaluations that several bidders wind up in a statistical tie. This is likely because where one might have scored higher than the other might on a particular category, the reverse might be true in another category. For this reason, and for the reasons stated before, this is not a scientific endeavor. At this stage, you are simply trying to get a relative ranking and make a first pass at a short list of bidders to continue in the process.

While the technical and managerial evaluations are taking place, the procurement manager will perform the commercial analysis. This will be used to see how well the bidders complied with the commercial part of the request.

While the price quoted would seem to be the overriding factor, there are many commercial terms that can significantly sway the analysis. Compliance to contract terms, change management procedures, and invoicing policies can impact significantly the overall project cost. An analysis of the life-cycle cost should also be done.

In performing a life-cycle cost analysis, the up-front cost is but one factor. The cost to operate and maintain the system or equipment must be considered. One vendor, for instance, might include motors that are less efficient than another's but will have a lower first cost. The projected electrical cost increase needs to be added to the analysis. Similarly, off-brand components in a network may be less reliable and more costly to maintain.

Such things as start-up or commissioning assistance, and ongoing technical support, can affect the analysis. If the higher priced proposal includes these items, while a lower priced one does not, then the net cost needs to be worked out. Freight from a distant location can also be significant, as can markup on third-party contracts and materials. If installation is required, how much is included, and what is the rate for extra hours and overtime?

As can be seen, the commercial evaluation involves more than just writing down the price. The criteria must be closely matched to the scope of work and contract terms to be of any value. Just because the procurement manager performs this analysis independently of the technical and managerial evaluations does not mean that the project team and other staff do not participate in the development and weighting of the evaluation criteria. On the contrary, consensus is needed on these items in order for the analysis to be accepted.

The purpose behind this setup is so that the project team can do their evaluation on the merits of the technical and management proposal, and not be influenced by the price. If the goal is to get the best for the project, then a low price may not be the best and could influence you into taking second best—especially if there is significant cost pressure on the project. It is also noteworthy that the price quoted is probably not the price that will ultimately be negotiated. Therefore, the influence of seeing the prices could be overstated. Also, the members of the technical and managerial teams should not feel slighted or believe that they are not trusted because they are excluded from the commercial analysis. This system indicates that quite the opposite is true.

Performing the analysis in this manner makes the technical and managerial teams' input far more valuable than in a more conventional situation. Most organizations have a policy that requires the lowest cost bidder be used unless there is a reason not to. If the noncommercial evaluation is done soundly, it will serve as justification for using someone other than the low bidder.

Specific Evaluation Criteria

Although the purpose of this section is to provide a generic framework for designing and conducting the bid evaluations, it will be helpful to provide a listing of some of the more common criteria that are frequently used to make these evaluations. Details of these criteria can be found in most good texts on the subject of subcontracts and procurement.

Technical and managerial criteria: Common technical and managerial criteria include:

- ▶ Equipment or systems compliance with RFP
- ▶ Technical capabilities
- ▶ Conceptual design
- ▶ Quality assurance program
- ▶ Training programs
- ▶ Work procedures
- ▶ Documentation procedures
- ▶ Compatibility with existing equipment or systems
- ▶ Spares and back-up availability
- ▶ Scheduling capability
- ▶ Reporting requirements
- ▶ Adequacy of facilities for project team visits
- ▶ Key personnel qualifications
- ▶ Other staff qualifications
- ▶ Safety and environmental programs (construction)

Commercial criteria: Some commercial criteria that should be considered are:

▶ Price

▶ Unit rates

▶ Markup on direct labor

▶ Incentive proposals

▶ Compliance with terms and conditions

▶ Cost of spares

▶ Cost of service

▶ Amount of service included

▶ Training cost

▶ Amount of training included

▶ Operating cost

▶ Freight

▶ Invoicing and payment terms

▶ Cost control program

▶ Warranties

▶ License cost

Many more could be developed given a specific proposal.

Analysis Technique for Proposals

The evaluation above can best be done if a detailed spreadsheet is prepared first. This spreadsheet should identify the relevant information regarding the proposed equipment or system, such as motor size, capacity of equipment, quality and quantity guaranteed, operating system used, and other relevant information that the bid should include.

The commercial spreadsheet could cover price, extras, freight, payment terms, warranty provisions, installation labor if separate, and the like.

This spreadsheet should list the vendors across the top and the relevant items down the side. It is handy to present the information this way because

> **A "sanity check" will tell you if a bidder has missed something**

you will have it in front of you when doing the evaluation. Remember that this spreadsheet is nonjudgmental. It simply organizes the information from the bids in a logical format so you can carry out the evaluations, which are by their nature judgmental. Once the bids are displayed this way it is also possible to do a "sanity check," seeing if the bids look reasonable for the amount of work that was solicited and how they compare to the estimate.

Post-Bid Meetings

For most major subcontracts, meetings with the bidders will be needed to clarify the proposal. The evaluation should form the basis for these meetings, and they may not be held with all bidders if the evaluation has allowed you to develop a short list. If this process has eliminated any bidders, the procurement manager should send them a letter thanking them for their participation but informing them that they are not going to be selected. This will allow the unsuccessful bidders to use their assets to pursue other projects. Most sellers bid more work than they can handle and are used to not getting it all.

The format for the post-bid meeting should be similar to the pre-bid, with the project manager chairing the session and calling on technical specialists as needed. The procurement manager should address contract and commercial issues. These meetings should be held with one bidder at a time.

It is not necessary to conduct the negotiation for the final contract at this time. The procurement manager should make it clear, however, that the negotiation process will follow soon, assuming that the responses to the issues raised in the post-bid are satisfactory. He should indicate that all areas of the proposal will be scrutinized, and that this post-bid meeting is to make sure that all parties have a clear understanding of the proposal as it relates to the requirements of the solicitation. The bidders should leave the meeting with a clear sense that the buyer expects them to improve their proposals.

Most procurement managers enjoy the game of cat-and-mouse that generally occurs in these meetings. They will use self-deprecating expressions such as "Well, I'm just an old country boy, but . . ." to let the bidders know that he fully understands the position he has put them in. Good procurement managers are a pleasure to observe. Just remember that this part is their show. Don't chime in unless you are asked to.

After the post-bid meetings the bidders will submit revised proposals, and the whole process happens again, although in a much more abbreviated fashion. You can then begin the negotiation process with one or more bidders.

CONTRACT ADMINISTRATION

You and the seller will finally agree on a contract to perform what was solicited and negotiated. This is commonly referred to as the "as-sold" proposal, meaning that the seller has made all of the adjustments and corrections needed to make the proposal agree with the contract. This is valuable, because the final contract will reference the "as-sold" proposal and, as such, it will become part of the contract. This is better than rewriting the proposal into the contract, since clerical errors could occur. Also, sellers are used to working with the format of their proposal, so their staff should be more familiar with the agreements reached.

Now that the contract has been signed, a whole other set of circumstances applies. This is no longer a give and take. There is now a legal document that outlines what both parties must do to fulfill their respective obligations.

In order to offer some help understanding this stage of the project, the following topics are included in this section:

▶ Contract terms and conditions

▶ Legal implications of actions by the parties

▶ Progress reporting and payment schedules

▶ Change management

▶ How to get what you paid for

Contract Terms and Conditions

Before getting into the litany of common contract terms and conditions, it must be pointed out that this is *not* a text on case law and that this information has been derived from published sources. Further, the writer is not a lawyer and

> **Always seek legal advice on a contract**

recommends that competent legal counsel be engaged for any serious use of this information.

Let's now delve into the terms and conditions, commonly called "mumbo jumbo" or "boilerplate."

For the most part, the particulars of the contract are based on the Uniform Commercial Code. Almost all states have subscribed to the UCC, which was developed in 1951 with the goal of establishing some uniformity in commercial work in the United States. The purpose of the contract is to formalize the agreement between the parties and make clear to what each has agreed. In order to do this, certain words are used that convey specific meanings given the section of the agreements in which they appear. These terms have been developed over the years and are based on the interpretations of the court system where the conflict was resolved. Over time, the meanings and intent of the terms were finalized.

> **"Term" refers to the subject. "Condition" refers to the particulars.**

"Term" refers to a topic heading, and "conditions" refers to the paragraphs that follow, outlining the specifics of the contract with regard to that particular term.

Some of the more common terms are:

Scope of work. This is the finalized scope that has been negotiated between the parties. It is sometimes referred to as the "as-sold scope." Many times it is included in the contract by reference rather than being totally spelled out. This may be because the "as-sold" is very lengthy, or technically complex, and errors could occur if the information was transcribed.

Specifications. Also generally included by reference by adding the specification index (with revision number!) to the contract.

Terms of payment. What payments will be made to whom, and when. This is where tying payments to a degree of completeness is covered. This approach is called progress payments, and should definitely be included in every contract. The conditions of the progress payments should prevent either party from causing the other undue financial burden.

Billing and invoicing information. There should be specific instructions as to when and where invoices should be sent, to whose attention they should be addressed, and what supporting documents are required in order for accounting to process the invoice.

Governing laws. This should indicate the parties' agreement as to which state's laws will apply in the event of a dispute.

Reporting and meeting requirements. This section should cover all *required* reports that must be submitted, the particulars of those submissions, and what project meetings should be anticipated and their location. Bear in mind that any reports or meetings asked for in addition to those identified in the contract may create an extra.

Indemnification. A fancy word meaning to hold harmless. This term is used by the buyer to protect him from damages that the seller may incur due to negligence or such things as patents and licenses.

Order of precedence. The order in which the various terms in the contract will be interpreted or enforced. For example, it is common to include a statement to the effect that, if there is a conflict between the drawings and the specifications, that the specifications (or vice versa) will take precedence. Precedence also generally dictates which of two conflicting items will prevail, even if they are not spelled out in the contract. This is called the Rule of Construction and discusses such things as words (twenty) over numbers (20), special provisions over general provisions, methods, definitions (industry specific over common), and a host of other terms.

Inspection. Generally there are provisions for inspection while the product is being made. This should be universally true for specialty engineered equipment, and checking of the progress and quality of software under development should be provided for as well. Along with this provision, *access to the site* should be defined.

Testing and acceptance. This relates to pre-arranged testing of the product and the buyer's acceptance of it. It may spell out what time frame the buyer has to accept the product without giving up the right of rejection. This applies especially in cases where the product was made using performance specifications. Time should be provided for the equipment to get up its learning curve before the testing is required. However, too much time leaves the seller in a bind, because the final payments are generally tied to acceptance. This is not always the case, and the final payment may be made with the final acceptance pending. Additional work to make the product perform correctly would be covered by the warranty clause.

Warranty. There are two kinds of warranties to be concerned about in contracts, express and implied. Express warranties are negotiated to cover explicit statements and provisions that the buyer can expect from the product. An implied warranty is one that can be assumed based on certain definitions in the law, such as the implied warranty of fitness for a particular purpose. Barring any disclaimers to the contrary, the buyer can be assured that a water pump will pump water, or that a fan will move air.

Express warranties void implied warranties on the points covered. The other provisions of the implied warranty still hold. Warranty provisions are frequently set in all CAPITAL letters to make them conspicuous.

Title. The title or ownership provision states how title will be trans-ferred, and who will own the title to such items as copyrights, patents, and intellectual property.

Change procedure. This critical section delineates the method whereby changes to certain parts of the contract are to be handled. Such items as schedule, scope, cost, and quality should be covered.

Remedies. Outlines the agreement between the buyer and seller as to what happens if one party or the other does not perform or *breaches* the contract. This covers such things as incentives and penalties and is where liquidated damages would be spelled out. Bear in mind that the term penalty has a specific meaning. Penalties imposed in the contract are not true penalties, or punishments, but are payments intended to make the other part whole, and should reflect the actual costs incurred as a result of the failure to perform.

Another form of remedy is *specific performance*, which simply means that the defaulting party must perform the specific activity that was spelled out in the contract. It is generally only enforced when some other type of compensation is inadequate.

The contract should also spell out how conflicts and differences are to be handled. (This will be covered later during contract closeout.)

Independent contractor. States that the seller is an independent con-tractor and therefore not an employee of the buyer. This is primarily a concern for taxes and benefits, but could have liability implications.

Agency. States who can act as a representative for each party. This is especially true in terms of controlling the work and making changes to the contract.

Termination. Details the circumstances under which either party may void the contract prior to its completion, and what actions would ensue, such as partial or full payments.

Time is of the essence. A statement that delivery is critical, and that failure to comply represents a breach of the contract. The term must be included to be in effect, and should not be if delivery is not critical. Delivery is always critical!

Force majeure. This is the famous "Act of God" clause stating that parties cannot be held liable for performance when prevented from doing so by forces outside of their control.

A contract can include many more terms and conditions. When the time comes to develop or interpret a contract, the purchasing and legal departments must be consulted.

Impact of Actions during the Contract

Along with a discussion of terms and conditions, there are several other definitions that may not be spelled out in the contract but which designate actions that may be taken during the contract that will have implications for the contract.

It is important to understand what these words mean because, for the most part, the staff handling the day-to-day activities of the project are not trained in the law or in procurement, but rather are technical and project people who have been trained in their specialties.

These definitions don't describe everything that can go wrong, just some of the more common occurrences.

Privity of contract. Privity of contract simply means that communications and directions to a subcontractor should only come from the other party in the contract. For example, assume that Buyer A has a contract with Contractor B to build a house. A and B have privity of contract with each other.

> **You must not direct the work of someone with whom you are not contracted**

All communications between them are spelled out in the contract, and A can legitimately direct B subject to the provisions of the contract. If B has hired Subcontractor C to do part of the work, B and C have privity, but A and C do not.

Constructive changes. This happens all the time. A buyer's representative on the project team "suggests" a change to a contractor with whom he has privity.

> **A change procedure will avoid problems**

The contractor does the work, then submits an extra because the work "suggested" caused him to redo some previously finished work. In most cases, the contractor has a legitimate claim. If someone in the buyer's organization that is not on the project team "suggests" a change, and the contractor does the work, he likely will get the extra as well. The challenge to this would be the level of detail in the agency clause of the contract. If the contractor had a "reasonable" expectation that the person was in authority, he would likely win.

Acceptance. What constitutes admission on your part that what the seller has provided is acceptable? In the case of performance specifications where verification or testing is to be done, the issue is fairly simple. When the product passes the test, it is acceptable. Using a product for a period of time without notification of rejection would likely constitute acceptance. Using a product beyond a time specified for acceptance constitutes acceptance. If the product is not OK, it should be rejected.

Progress Reporting and Payments

Many contracts call for payments to be made as the work progresses. This is to prevent the seller from having to fund the entire project, as many are not big enough to do so. If this is the case, though, the cost of financing the project should be an allowable cost that should be reimbursed.

Progress payments are generally tied to milestones on the project schedule. This method is called the schedule of values, and ties payments to progress. In the case of building a house it could be something like:

10 percent down at the signing of the contract

10 percent when the lot is cleared

20 percent when the foundation and undergrounds pass inspection

20 percent when the walls and roof are on (dried-in), and so on

Sometimes the appliances and air-conditioning equipment are paid for as they are delivered. A certain portion of the money would be held back to ensure contract completion.

Given that watching a house go up allows for a rather quick assessment of progress on the job, the question of just how much progress has been made is fairly straightforward. This is generally not true on big or complex projects, or on intellectual property projects. There must be some mechanism for understanding what progress to pay for.

There is no magic answer as to how to do this. By sticking to the basics of project management, the following methods should be adequate:

Progress reports. The use of progress reporting should be spelled out in the contract, and the details and forms of reports need to be identified early in the contracting exercise. Since all projects are different, no single format will suffice, but the basics—man-hours expended, materials received, quantities of material installed, and the like—are needed.

The progress report must be provided in a timely manner in order that payments can be made. The report should be distributed per the contract.

Schedule updates. The schedule that has been agreed to in the contract should be updated on a frequent and regular basis. You should require the seller to provide such an update with the progress report. It should be in a commercial software program format so that you can analyze it for discrepancies or errors, and also to anticipate future problems. You should ensure that someone on the team can use the software.

Status meetings. It is the conventional wisdom that everyone detests status meetings, and that all status meetings are a waste of time. This is

> **Don't tell your life story at a status meeting**

probably true in most organizations, because the status meetings are not conducted in a proper fashion. All too often, the status meeting is run like a staff meeting, where each person can inform the others as to what is happening on his project. A proper status meeting has a fixed agenda, and reports are given by various groups as to the current state of the part of the project that they control. At a minimum, the presenters should include:

► Project manager (gives introduction)

► Safety

► Environmental

► Engineering

► Procurement

► Accounting

► Implementation or construction

► Buyer's personnel, as applicable

Each presenter should provide an overview of their progress, using schedules, man-hours, spending, material receipts, earned value, or other recognizable indicators. They should also provide a two-week preview, or some indicator of what is coming, so that others can plan their work as well.

The length of the meetings will depend on the project, but it is unlikely much real discussion can happen in less than two hours.

As time consuming as the preparation and conduct of the meeting may seem, no real substitute exists for an effective status meeting. Faceless reports do not allow for the give-and-take and ultimate agreement that can be derived from a status meeting.

Change Management

The scope of a project should be written such that all parties agree to what is and is not included, using the basic assumptions that were used in defining the scope. The work breakdown structure (WBS) should be used to generate the lowest-level work packages practical. These in turn should be used to generate the estimate and be the basis for the schedule. Assuring that all of these are in place should minimize changes to the project.

It is inherent in project work that changes are going to occur. These changes might be from outside causes, such as regulatory agencies, or from inside sources, as in the case of a requirement change for the product after the project has been started. The most common type of change, however, is caused by a failure of management and the project team to fully understand and agree to why the project is being performed, and what it entails. There are times when this is done with malice aforethought, in which case the project team has little choice but to accept the change. Also, not all changes are bad. Often the project will not function as well without the change. Another common cause of changes is ambiguity on the part of the buyer when writing specifications.

Once a subcontract has been signed, changes need to be made following a formal change procedure. Typical changes at this stage have to do with scope, schedule, and cost. Without getting into the specifics of each type of change, the following steps should be taken on any change:

A formal change procedure must be written that outlines who has the authority to make changes, and what procedures must be followed to affect

Develop a discipline to use the change management process

the change.

A defined change committee should be set up on larger projects. It is common for the committee to be staffed by senior people who are not on the project team but are familiar with the project.

Each change request must indicate the cost and schedule impacts of the change.

Except in an emergency, the seller should do no work until the procurement group has issued a change order.

Changes should be handled expeditiously to avoid unnecessary delays and even more changes.

To protect against changes that creep into the project, the project manager should do the following:

▶ Read and understand the contract

▶ Keep and circulate detailed notes of telephone conversations

▶ Keep a diary detailing the events of each day

▶ Ensure in writing that the seller knows who has the authority to direct the work.

▶ Circulate minutes of meetings to all team members and sellers

▶ Follow the formal change procedure yourself

One last note on change orders. A properly executed change order is your friend. It authorizes you to spend money that you are not currently authorized to spend.

> **Change orders can be your friend**

Many of the changes that occur are well thought out and for the good of the project, and are approved as such by senior management.

Getting What You Paid For

Obviously, the first step in *getting* what you paid for is *knowing* what you paid for. Surprisingly, this is probably the most difficult part in getting a product delivered that performs as it should.

Everyone on the project team must have a full and complete knowledge of the scope and specifications. If performance specifications are used, the basis for them and the testing or inspection criteria need to be established up-front and shared with the seller. Often, the performance specifications will reference some standard testing procedure. This can be either an industry standard or a general standard, such as ANSI.

Beyond the need to have and understand the knowledge required to ensure that the product delivered by the seller meets the terms of the contract, there are several tools and techniques that can be used *during* the project to make sure you get what you paid for. Some of these are:

Product progress reports. Not to be confused with the progress reports needed for a payment application, these reports are more technical in nature. The report could show intermediate quality testing, such as how much of the code has been debugged or how many I/O (input/output) points have been identified, or the final testing of a sub-assembly, such as a hydraulic unit.

The items of importance in the progress report should be identified and agreed to between you and seller early in the project. These reports should be included in the project schedule.

Third-party testing. The use of third-party testing is common in many industries. An independent laboratory is hired by the buyer to ensure that intermediate and final assemblies meet the prescribed standards. For example, an inspector might be hired to ensure that all of the bolts in a steel building are properly tightened; further than that, it is common to have representative samples of the bolts tested by a lab to verify that they meet the required strength characteristics. Testing the concrete mix and the placement of reinforcing would also be examples.

Specialists could be hired to test and approve electronic assemblies that are going into a controls system. Critical items could be sent to an outside lab for capacity testing. Almost every industry can make use of contracted auditors to act as a control on the product being supplied.

Bonds. The use of a bond to ensure that the project is complete is another tool to make sure that the seller delivers the product ordered. In a bonding situation, you buy a form of insurance policy, a bond, which guarantees that the

> **Bonds are a form of insurance**

project will be completed. This type of insurance is called a performance bond. It does not specify who will complete the project, but rather provides the funds for someone to deliver in the case where the original seller cannot.

Other types of bonds commonly used are the bid bond and the payment bond. A bid bond may be required of all bidders on a project. This type of bond guarantees that the successful bidder will sign a contract and enter into the necessary arrangements to supply the product. Unlike a performance bond, the bid bond expires when the contract is signed. If the successful bidder backs out, the bid bond will pay the difference for the next lowest bidder to complete the contract.

Payment bonds are used to insure that the primary seller pays his bills for materials and other subcontractors. A maintenance bond is actually an extended warranty on the product.

Most government contracts will include some or all of these types of bonds. General industry's use of bonds has declined over time, due to the fact that the administrative costs are high, and the bonds don't guarantee the quality of the work by an incompetent seller.

Shop inspections. The use of shop inspections for manufactured equipment is probably the best way to ensure that you are getting what you ordered. This is due to the fact that the seller knows that you are coming, and that you know what you are looking for. Don't disappoint them! Nothing will damage your credibility more than showing up for a shop inspection ill prepared and ignorant about what you are inspecting.

Shop inspections can be expensive, as they generally involve travel to the seller's production facility, or a staging facility if the seller has one, such as in the case of large controls systems. Given the global economy, the inspection may require overseas travel and the attendant living expenses. In some cases, the use of a local inspector, such as an engineering firm, could be used. Still, I prefer that you, the buyer, go if for no other reason than your own education.

If the product being inspected is to be installed during an outage, such as in the case of a computer system or software for a critical activity like banking or healthcare, or on the outage of major production equipment, the shop inspection needs to be expanded to cover not only the details of the product itself, but the planning needed for a timely installation. Provisions for temporarily running both systems in parallel could be made during the inspection. Large assemblies could be match marked so that they could be put back together more efficiently. Cabling should similarly be identified and marked.

A shop inspection report must be prepared when the inspection has been completed so that everyone that has an interest—including especially the installation forces—will know the status and what they need to do to assist.

CONTRACT CLOSEOUT

The need to properly close out the contract cannot be overemphasized. Not only does a legal agreement exist, which must be completed, but also you need to wrap up all the details.

Generally, you, as project manager, are responsible for seeing that all necessary steps have been taken to complete the project. However, there are times you might be reassigned prior to the final closing of the project. Therefore, the notes and daily diary mentioned before become even more valuable.

Common activities during the final closeout of the project include:

> **Resolution of claims.** Most misunderstandings should have been
> resolved during the course of the execution of the contract; how-
> ever, some disputes are held off by mutual agreement until the end
> of the contract. Other claims don't appear until the work is fin-
> ished. Contract language to the effect that "all disputes must be

brought to the attention of the buyer . . ." may work, but there are still likely to be claims to be settled. Remember that most claims, like most changes, are caused by poorly worded agreements or poorly communicated expectations.

There are basically four means available to resolve disputes and settle claims. These are, in order of desirability:

▶ *Negotiation.* The parties work out their differences and reach some amicable accord.

> **There are four ways to settle a dispute**

▶ *Mediation.* The buyer and seller voluntarily bring in a third party to assist the process of reaching an agreement.

▶ *Arbitration.* The buyer and seller agree to abide by the decision of a third party that will hear both sides and render a decision. Arbitration can be voluntary or compulsory and is generally called for in the contract.

▶ *Litigation.* The case goes to court and everybody loses but the lawyers!

Deliverables. All projects have some deliverables to support the product that was ordered. In most cases, there will be such things as operating and maintenance manuals, as built or as wired drawings, which reflect changes to the design during installation, source code if applicable, and any number of industry-specific items that are called out in the contract.

In the case of documentation needed to train employees on the use and repair of the product, or spare parts to support the product when it goes into service, the delivery of these items should be the basis for a progress payment. This often proves to be very difficult arrange, however.

Retainage and final payment. Throughout the project, accounting has held back a portion of each invoice in the form of retainage. The purpose of retainage is to make sure that the seller has an incentive to complete the project. In most cases, the retainage represents the seller's profit. It is also there to allow the buyer to

> **Be sure and get the final paperwork before paying the final bill**

get any unfinished work done (see litigation, above).

Once the seller has complied with the terms of the contract, including deliverables and releases, he will apply for his final payment. You must satisfy yourself that everything is in proper order before authorizing the final payment. In the case where there is a performance test after a period on the learning curve, a partial release of retainage is common.

The accounting department will likely be the last group to close the project, as they have to process all of the final invoices that trickle in and close the project to the general ledger and asset accounts, to begin depreciation.

Warranties. The term of the warranty generally begins with the acceptance and final payment, but may begin at different times for "bought–out" equipment from third-party subcontractors. Frequently, these warranties state that the warranty is active from the date the item is put in service, or six months after delivery. This is because the third party has no control over when the item will actually be used.

You need to see that the registrations for warranties are completed and returned to the seller (or warrantor, in the case of third-party equipment). This is not necessary to put the warranty in force, but is valuable for updates and recalls.

Post-project review. Alternately called lessons learned or post-completion audits, this exercise brings together the members of your project team and all sellers' representatives for a comprehensive review of the project. Interviews are held with the sellers' key personnel, as well as those in your organization that use the product. You should develop standard format interview forms so that the participants all get a fair chance at commenting on the project.

Often the project is such that it is impractical to have all participants sit in on the presentation, but they should at least get a set of notes from the event.

In times past, this type of audit was considered a witch-hunt and concentrated primarily on cost overruns. Thankfully, that is not the case in most organizations anymore.

CONCLUSION

The topic of how to manage contracts, from selection through contract development and implementation, is a critical part of your job. While there are specialists available in all pertinent areas, the need for an in-depth understanding of the necessary procedures and processes cannot be overestimated.

The legal nature of a contract makes this especially important. You must learn and follow the "rules of the game" so that misunderstandings can be avoided and the project can run smoothly. I hope that the information presented in this chapter will be of value in making every contract successful—and fun.

AREAS OF INTEREST IN THIS CHAPTER

The following are some of the key elements covered in this chapter and in the PMBOK:

- ▶ Ethical behavior
- ▶ The elements of the PMBOK procurement cycle (memorize these!):
    - ■ Procurement planning—what to obtain (make or buy)
    - ■ Solicitation planning—identify product details and determine sources
    - ■ Solicitation—the act of obtaining quotes
    - ■ Source selection—the process of determining the right supplier
    - ■ Contract administration—managing the relationship

- Contract closeout—finalizing the deal and resolving conflicts

▶ Elements of a contract

- Offer

- Acceptance

- Consideration

- Legal purpose

- Competent parties

▶ Contract types, advantages and disadvantages of each

- Fixed price

- Cost reimbursable

  ✓ Cost plus fixed fee

  ✓ Cost plus a percentage (more risky)

- Unit rate (also called time and material)

- Incentives for good performance can be added (bonus)

- Penalties for poor performance can also be added (penalty or liquidated damages)

▶ Forms of solicitation

- RFP

- RFQ

- IFB

- Noncompetitive forms of solicitation

  ✓ Sole source

  ✓ Single source

- ► Procurement plan

- ► Procurement documents

  - ■ Plans

  - ■ Specifications

  - ■ Standard contract (boilerplate)

  - ■ Terms and conditions

- ► Pre-bid and post-bid meetings

- ► Proposal evaluation and award

- ► Contract administration pitfalls

  - ■ Privity

  - ■ Constructive change

  - ■ Unintentional acceptance

- ► Change management

- ► Contract closeout

  - ■ Resolution of conflicts

    - ✓ Negotiation

    - ✓ Mediation

    - ✓ Arbitration

    - ✓ Litigation

  - ■ Lessons learned

SAMPLE QUESTIONS: CHAPTER 12—SELECT THE *BEST* ANSWER

1. What are the three basic contract types identified in the PMBOK?

    A. Negotiated, fixed fee, blanket order

    B. Fixed fee, cost reimbursable, incentive

    C. Fixed fee, time and material, unit rate

    D. Fixed price, cost reimbursable, time and material

2. Which of the following is not an element of a contract?

    A. Consideration

    B. Competent parties

    C. Offer

    D. Negotiation

3. What is a RFP?

    A. A modified form of a fixed-fee contract

    B. A form of solicitation that asks for skilled input to solve a problem

    C. A form of change order

    D. None of the above

4. What is meant by privity?

    A. That the contents of the contract are secret

    B. It is a form of bonus/penalty arrangement

    C. It is a term that describes contractual relationships

    D. It has to do with warranties

5. When should the evaluation criteria for proposals be developed?

   A. During the solicitation planning step

   B. Only after the proposals have been received

   C. In the procurement planning step

   D. As part of the make-or-buy decision

6. Who should lead the contract negotiation phase?

   A. The project manager

   B. The accounting representative

   C. The functional manager

   D. The procurement manager

7. What is an advantage to the buyer of a fixed-price contract?

   A. It requires less work on the buyer's behalf to develop the bid documents

   B. It puts the risk on the seller

   C. It is easier to make changes during execution

   D. Work can begin before all of the project documents are in place

8. What are liquidated damages?

   A. Part of a time and material contract

   B. An evaluation technique

   C. An agreed-to penalty for missing a project milestone

   D. A form of insurance policy

9. What is a make-or-buy analysis?

   A. A method of determining elements that will be part of the project

   B. A method of determining elements that must be obtained from outside

   C. A method of determining the type of contract to use

   D. A method of identifying the bidders

10. Why is an internal contract not a real contract?

   A. It is a real contract

   B. Most organizations do not allow internal contracts

   C. Someone higher up in the organization can void the agreement

   D. None of the above

11. Which of the following contract types puts the most risk on the *buyer*?

   A. Fixed fee (FF)

   B. Cost reimbursable with a fixed fee (CPFF)

   C. Negotiated price

   D. Cost reimbursable with a percentage fee (CPPF)

12. What are terms and conditions?

   A. Part of the proposal evaluation

   B. A listing of definitions that apply to the contract

   C. Part of the negotiation process

   D. The procurement plan

13. What are the three common types of solicitation identified in the PMBOK?

    A. IFB, RFP, RFQ

    B. FF, CP, T&M

    C. Sole source, RFQ, budget quote

    D. Form of proposal, IFB, T&M

14. What is meant by constructive change?

    A. Change will help the project

    B. One party assumes that the other party is honest

    C. One party assumes that the other has the authority to make changes

    D. It is a "no cost" change order

15. What are the four types of dispute resolution?

    A. Discussion, negotiation, mediation, arbitration

    B. Arbitration, litigation, accommodation, amelioration

    C. Listening, evaluating, negotiating, cooperating

    D. Negotiation, mediation, arbitration, litigation

16. Which of the following is not an element of a contract?

    A. Legal purpose

    B. Offer

    C. Negotiation

    D. Competent parties

17. Why should bids not be opened until the specified time?

   A.   The supplier has the right to modify or withdraw their bid until the specified time

   B.   It is against the law in most government work

   C.   To do so might compromise the bid evaluation

   D.   All of the above

18. A time and material contract could be used when:

   A.   All documents and specifications have been completed

   B.   Quantities are unknown but a rate per unit is desirable

   C.   More than one seller has submitted a bid

   D.   The buyer demands a warranty

19. Why are incentives (bonus/penalty) used?

   A.   To protect the seller

   B.   To protect the client

   C.   To reward good performance and penalize poor performance

   D.   To help in the evaluation process

20. Detailed specifications:

   A.   Describe how a product must perform

   B.   Describe how a product must be made

   C.   Are the same as standards

   D.   Are not used in a time and materials contract

Chapter 13

Professional Responsibility

The topic of professional responsibility was added to the PMP exam in March 2002. As such, there is nothing in the PMBOK to help you prepare for the exam. A study of the PMI Web site does reveal several reference sources, and the Web site also has a practice examination

New topic . . . not in the PMBOK!

that has questions related to professional responsibility. In this chapter I examine each of the referenced materials so that you can gain a more in-depth understanding of the topic.

First, though, let me emphasize several points. Some of the material covered in professional responsibility includes material that is already in the other knowledge areas of the PMBOK. Many of the topics relate to cost, schedule, and so on, but from a situational perspective. For exam-

Questions cross over processes and knowledge areas

ple, a question may ask what you should do if you discover a missing piece of work that, if left undone, would increase the favorable variance at the end of the project.

This is a cost or WBS question in those knowledge areas, but is an ethical one in professional responsibility. Also, the professional responsibility topic expands the knowledge base by focusing on the PMI Code of Conduct (which is found on page 22 of the *Certification Handbook*), the PMI PMP, and a variety of topics on ethics, legality, professional behavior, judgment, and cultural differences.

PMI CODE OF CONDUCT

As mentioned, this is on page 22 of the *Certification Handbook*. You need to read it carefully and follow it as a guide in your exam prep and professional life. Briefly, the topics covered are:

I.   Responsibility to the Profession

    A.   Comply with all organization rules and policies

        1.   Provide accurate information to PMI regarding the PMP certification program. In other words, tell the truth and don't try to embellish your Experience Verification forms.

        2.   Given that you have the facts, you are obliged to report code of conduct violations by PMP members in the project management field.

        3.   You are expected to cooperate with PMI during ethics violations.

        4.   You are obliged to report potential conflicts of interest or appearances of impropriety to owners, clients, customers,

❧ ❧ Code of Conduct: you agree to this when you apply for certification ❧ ❧

etc. Your client has the right to know if you have a personal interest in a potential supplier.

B.   Candidate professional practice

   1.   You are responsible for providing accurate and complete representations concerning qualifications, experience, and performance of services claimed.

   2.   You agree to comply with the laws and standards of the country in which you are practicing the profession.

C.   Advance the profession

   1.   You have a responsibility to recognize and respect the intellectual property of others, and to act in a competent and truthful manner in your dealings.

2. You have a responsibility to support the Code and to ensure that other PMPs understand and comply with the Code.

II. Responsibility to customers and the public

A. Relating to qualifications, experience, and ability

1. You must be truthful and accurate as to representations or advertisements to your clients about your background and abilities. You also have the same obligation when preparing contract documents.

> **Responsibility to the profession and the public**

2. You have the obligation to satisfy the scope and objectives (not always the same thing!) of your professional services.

3. Respect the confidentiality of any information provided or generated during the course of a project, and beyond, until authorized by the client.

B. Conflicts of interest and other prohibited forms of conduct

1. You must act to ensure that your work does not involve a conflict of interest for your client. You must also resist pressures that might call your professional judgment into question.

2. You have an obligation to refrain from accepting gifts or other forms of inducement. This must be tempered with sensitivity to the laws and customs of the country where the service is provided.

This last point will be expanded upon when I discuss the cultural aspects of professional responsibility.

PMI PMP ROLE DELINEATION STUDY

In 2000, PMI commissioned the Project Management Professional Role Delineation Survey to ascertain if the exam actually covered the knowledge and duties that a competent project manager should know. Six "domains' were identified. The first five were the standard PMBOK process areas of:

▶ Initiating

▶ Planning

▶ Executing

Remember these?

▶ Controlling

▶ Closing

A sixth domain was identified that recognized that professional responsibility was not fully covered. (A copy of this study may be purchased from PMI.)

There are five subtopics to the professional responsibility domain:

▶ Ensure integrity

▶ Contribute to the knowledge base

Professional responsibility domain topics

▶ Apply professional knowledge

▶ Balance stakeholder interests

▶ Respect differences

Each of these is linked to the other processes and knowledge areas by identifying tasks, knowledge, and skill. The Role Delineation Survey is a copyrighted publication, so I am not going to reproduce it here (see C 1 in the Code of Conduct above!). However, I can offer a bit of explanation for each of these subtopics, and really do recommend that you purchase your own copy, or see if your local library or PMI chapter has one that you can borrow.

> **You need to get the Role Delineation Survey to get to a complete understanding of the topic**

▶ *Ensure integrity.* This means that you will adhere to the legal and ethical requirements to protect all involved. To do this, you must know and understand the various laws and standards and have the judgment needed to apply them

▶ *Contribute to the knowledge base.* This means that you have an obligation to share your knowledge, best practices, lessons learned, and research to improve the profession and your colleagues. To accomplish this, it is important that you understand the knowledge base, the appropriate communities within the profession, and the methods of disseminating information. Your skill in communicating and your ability to exercise judgment as it relates to confidential or proprietary methods are important in this. By judgment, I mean that there may be methods developed for a particular client that must not be shared without permission.

▶ *Apply professional knowledge.* This relates to your professional competence. You need to be introspective and define your needs through self-assessment, your learning style, and your areas of interest. You should develop the insight that lets you see what your areas of deficiency are and pursue training and education that meets your particular style.

▶ *Balance stakeholder interests.* Your task as a project manager is to assist your client, and other interested parties, in developing solutions that attempt to balance the competing needs of these groups. Conflict-resolution techniques, negotiations training, and judgment are key skill areas

▶ *Respect differences.* In this day and age, understanding of ethic, cultural, and personal differences is not an option. Globalization and worldwide collaboration are here and must be dealt with. You should understand that different team members will have varied backgrounds, norms, mores, and preferred communications methods. Some will prefer a long time to reach a consensus, and others will want to charge on. Your skill at controlling the group dynamic and being understanding of and empathetic to others' differences will be key in success in this domain.

CULTURAL ASPECTS OF PROFESSIONAL RESPONSIBILITY

As you find yourself in the world of global project management, it is critical that you understand the impact that cultural differences will have on your ability to

Understanding cultural differences is important

succeed—and survive, for that manner! You do not have to travel overseas to require this awareness. Increasingly, detailed engineering, coding, and such are being done in countries other than the United States. Major shifts in manufacturing are taking place, so it is likely that somewhere along the line you are going to be confronted by a situation that means you need to understand cultural and ethnic differences.

PMI recommends three books on the subject:

Global Literacies: Lessons on Business Leadership and National Cultures. Rosen, Digh, and Phillips; Simon and Schuster, 2000

Doing Business Internationally: The Guide to Cross-Cultural Success. Blake, Walker; McGraw-Hill Professional Book Group, 1995

The Cultural Dimension of International Business. Ferraro; Prentice Hall, 1997

All are good references that emphasize the need to understand other cultures from their perspective. Rosen, et al. summarizes this need well by defining four "global literacies":

A good synopsis of the topic

▶ Personal Literacy: Understanding and Valuing Yourself

▶ Social Literacy: Engaging and Challenging Others

▶ Business Literacy: Focusing and Mobilizing Your Organization

▶ Cultural Literacy: Valuing and Leveraging Cultural Differences

I am going to recommend a fourth:

Do's and Taboos Around the World. (SIC) Axtell; John Wiley and Sons, 1993

I have been fortunate in my career to travel the world extensively, and have found this book to be a tremendous help. One of its topics is gift giving, a phenomenon that is almost totally foreign to Americans, since we do little of it in our professional lives. Many cultures con-

Gift giving is deeply ingrained in many cultures

sider gift giving not as a bribe but as the first step in developing a relationship. Of course, there are cultures where an actual bribe is not only accepted, but is needed to conduct business.

I was traveling to Indonesia with a colleague and our host, Mr. K. We were designing and constructing a chemical plant on the outskirts of Surabaya, on the island of Java. When we arrived at passport control, the line was 50 people long and not moving at all. Mr. K. collected our passports, inserted R 50,000 (Rupiah—about $8.00), and barged to the head of the line. A little arm-waving and

> **A "service fee" is not really a bribe . . . it is a cost of doing business**

heated discussion later, we were escorted past everyone else and were on our way! Mr. K. pointed out that, as Americans, we were expected to pay a "service fee" to arrange for expedited action. This was not a bribe, per se, but a cost of doing business.

Another important aspect of dealing with other cultures is to recognize that people from the United States and some European countries are about the only ones that expect to conduct business on the first (or even second) meeting. My time in China demonstrated that the Chinese prefer to have social interactions, such as a dinner that lasts for hours, before getting down to business. This is not only their cultural

Patience is a virtue when dealing with other cultures

history; it is good negotiating. They learn a lot about who is really in charge from these sessions, and they keep the Americans on edge about not making progress!

Further, their negotiating technique is to keep delaying, knowing full well that you have a plane to catch. If you reschedule, they will delay further. Remember, we have been at this for a few hundred years. They have been at it for 3,000!

These are but a few examples of why you must learn the ways of those in different cultures and respect those differences, whether it is you are they who are visiting. Time and the Internet have blurred many of the aspects that used to make foreign travel so foreign. McDonald's is everywhere, and most clothes in your suitcase

> **Make it a point to enjoy learning about other cultures ... they will respect you for it**

were not made in the United States. What has not changed is the appreciation and gratitude on the part of your foreign visitors and associates when they feel you have tried to learn something about them and their country. Besides, it is a lot of fun!

CONCLUSION

In this chapter I have outlined the documents and publications that PMI suggests you study for this part of the exam. There may be 25 to 30 questions on the exam about professional responsibility. Many of them will be situational and associated with the other processes and knowledge areas. I recommend that you obtain at least some of the referenced material for further study, as copyright provisions do not allow me to supply it for your study.

AREAS OF EMPHASIS IN THIS CHAPTER

The following are some of the key elements covered in this chapter and in the references given by PMI:

▶ Professional responsibility is not covered in the PMBOK

▶ Three general topics are involved

  ■ PMI Code of Conduct

    • Governs your actions and obligations as a PMP

    • Contains two general topics

      ✓ Responsibility to the profession

      ✓ Responsibility to customers and the public

  ■ Role Delineation Survey

    • Conducted in 2000

    • Identified professional responsibility as a domain not well covered

    • There are five parts to the professional responsibility domain

      ✓ Ensure integrity

      ✓ Contribute to the knowledge base

      ✓ Advance professional knowledge

      ✓ Balance stakeholder interests

      ✓ Respect differences

    • Each of these are further broken down into three subsets

      ✓ What is the *task?*

      ✓ What *knowledge* is needed?

      ✓ What *skills* are needed to succeed?

- Cultural aspects of professional responsibility

  - Globalization

  - Cultural Differences

  - Reference material

SAMPLE QUESTIONS: CHAPTER 13—SELECT THE *BEST* ANSWER

1. As project manager on an environmental remediation project, you discover that a small amount of material has been left in the ground. The site has been backfilled and seeded, and the contractor is preparing to leave. The material has been determined to be moderately hazardous. What should be your course of action?

    A. Notify the project sponsor

    B. Allow the contractor to demobilize

    C. Negotiate with the environmental regulators

    D. Ignore this minor fault

2. You are in a foreign land, and are feeling uncomfortable about handling yourself. What is this called?

    A. Jet lag

    B. Culture shock

    C. Time delay

    D. Xenophobia

3. Your contract calls for you getting a bonus of 5 percent of the favorable variance. You find that a substitute for a material specified will save $20,000 with no noticeable difference in performance. What should you do?

    A. Make the change

B. Continue on without making the change

C. Notify the project sponsor that you can save them money

D. Have purchasing re-bid the item

4. During a visit to the site of the project of one of your company's other project managers, you observe what you think is illegal behavior on the part of one of the project engineers. Your preferred course of action would be:

   A. Notify the police

   B. Notify your superior

   C. Confront the individual

   D. Ignore the infraction; it is not your project

5. Which of the following best describes the proper mood for international negotiations?

   A. Mutual trust

   B. Divisiveness

   C. Unease

   D. Bullying

6. Different standards of conduct in cultures are known as:

   A. Laws

   B. Folkways

   C. Habits

   D. Mores

7. According to the PMI Code of Conduct, to which group do you have responsibility?

    A. Other PMPs

    B. The public

    C. The customer

    D. All of the above

8. In order to satisfy the client, you must define:

    A. Wants

    B. Likes

    C. Needs

    D. Desires

9. When confronted with a request for a "service charge" or "facilitation fee" by a low-level official in a foreign country, you should:

    A. Call the United States Embassy

    B. Call the local police

    C. Call the project sponsor

    D. Pay the charge and include the information in your daily diary

10. Which of the following represents hurdles to be overcome in global business?

    A. Language differences

    B. Time differences

    C. Cultural differences

    D. All of the above

Chapter 14

Preparing for the PMP Exam

In this final chapter of our PMP preparation book, I will cover the details concerning actually preparing for the certification process. I will cover everything from applying for certification, through preparing for the actual exam, what to expect on the day of the exam, and finally how to maintain your certification once you have achieved it. I will also review a few test-taking tips that you may find helpful.

I realize that if you have read this far into the book, and are serious about becoming certified, you probably already know a lot of this information. Still, a little review can't hurt!

APPLYING FOR CERTIFICATION

Everything you need to know about applying for certification can be found on the Project Management Institute (PMI) web page at www.pmi.org. Specifically, the PMP *Certification Handbook* can be accessed under the "Certification" tab on the home page. The address for this book is:

http://www.pmi.org/prod/groups/public/documents/info/PDC_PMPHandbook.pdf

Bear in mind that this address may change over time, but the PMI web page is easily searchable.

There are two categories of application:

▶ Category 1: the applicant has a bachelor's degree or equivalent and has accumulated 4,500 hours of project experience over 36 nonoverlapping months within the past 6 years.

▶ Category 2: the applicant has a high-school education or equivalent and has accumulated 7,500 hours of project experience over 60 nonoverlapping months within the past 8 years.

Keep in mind that these hours do not have to be logged as "the project manager." PMI recognizes a wide range of project roles that satisfy this requirement.

The basic requirements for applying for certification are as follows:

▶ Thirty-five hours of professional education in project management completed before the application is submitted. There is no timeline for this requirement, but it must cover the five process areas and be documented on a form in the *Certification Handbook*.

▶ Completed application showing educational background. Note that by signing the application, you are certifying that you have read the Certificate and Candidate Agreement and Release on page 12 of the *Handbook*. It is a bunch of legalese saying that nothing is PMI's fault!

▶ Experience Verification forms documenting the required hours of experience appropriate to the category selected.

▶ Pay $405 application fee.

You can apply on-line or by mail.

Once you have applied, you can expect a reply within 20 days. Assuming your application is accepted, you will receive a letter authorizing you to contact the testing center for a sitting appointment. The letter is good for six months, although one six-month extension may be granted. The first six months is plenty of time, so don't think about the extension. I recommend that you arrange your test date soon after getting your letter, for two reasons:

▶ The test centers have a finite number of spaces, and they administer many other exams as well as the PMP test.

▶ By setting your date you will establish a milestone in your schedule for becoming certified. Procrastination is not a desirable characteristic for a project manager!

Thompson Prometrics currently administers the exam. Complete details about scheduling the exam will be in the letter.

TAKING THE EXAM

You will be assigned a date, time, and place for the exam. There are many sites nationwide, so you will probably go to one in your locale. You should find the site before your test day, and arrive 15 minutes early on your appointed day. Once exam time has arrived, latecomers will not be admitted.

You will be required to show two forms of identification, one of them a picture ID. The names on the identification cards must be identical to the name on the application and authorization letter, so make sure that you have done your part *and* that PMI has transcribed the information correctly.

You will not be allowed to take anything into the test with you, except a sweater or jacket. Electronic devices, personal calculators, and cell phones are not allowed, so leave them at home or in your car. The receptionist and site personnel will not take responsibility for them.

A calculator, paper, and pencils will be at your test station. Test sites tend to be cool, to keep people awake, so a jacket would be a good idea. I have had people tell me that they were allowed to bring a snack and leave it in the lobby with the receptionist, and I have been told exactly the opposite. I suggest that you eat before you go and skip the snack. You will only be allowed to leave the testing room for breaks; however, you must stay in the building. Generally, restrooms are in the lobby, not in the testing area.

The test site typically has a dozen or more booths in one large room. There will be people taking nursing exams, teacher certifications, and any number of other tests. Theirs may be longer or shorter than yours. You should avoid letting them disturb you; nor should you disturb others.

The Test Itself

You will be given a 15-minute orientation on the equipment that you will use to take the test. This is typically a short lesson on some subject and a few questions to get you used to the format.

The PMP test consists of 200 multiple-choice questions. Each question has four possible answers. Some questions may ask you to fill in a blank, but most will be of the types that I will describe later. You have four hours, not counting the 15-minute orientation, to complete the exam. These four hours include any breaks that you take, so I recommend that you limit your fluid intake the morning of the test!

The testing system itself works well. You sit in front of a monitor and control the test with a mouse. When a question appears on the screen, you simply click the answer that you want recorded. If you are unsure, you can click a box that says "Mark for Later Review" or some such wording; after you finish answering the other questions you can return to these. Actually, you can go back to them at any time, which is good because a subsequent question may remind you of the correct answer to one that you had marked for review.

You will be given an opportunity to review all of your answers before you conclude. Once you have decided you are through, you click on the button that so indicates. The computer will automatically click this button after the four hours elapse, whether or not you have completed the exam. This does not mean you failed . . . you may have answered enough questions correctly even if you did not get to them all.

A moment later (although it seems longer!) the word PASS or FAIL will appear on the screen. The testing staff will also get this indication. They will transmit the information to PMI. Since I am confident that by studying this book and some of the Suggested Readings you will pass, for all intents and purposes you are now a PMP!

As I said, there are 200 questions on the exam. It takes 137 correct answers to pass. PMI has produced a distribution that shows what percentage of questions come from each of the five process areas plus professional responsibility. This breakdown is shown in the following table.

Process Area	Percent of Questions	Number of Questions
Initiating	8.5	17
Planning	23.5	47
Executing	23.5	47
Controlling	23.0	46
Closing	7.0	14
Professional Responsibility	14.5	29
Total Questions	100.0	200

Details of this breakdown are covered on PMI's Web site. The following Web address contains the information:

http://www.pmi.org/prod/groups/public/documents/info/PDC_PMPExamDetails.asp

There are also sample questions from each process area on the Web site.

The test questions were written by PMPs to ensure accuracy, and were reviewed by testing experts to ensure validity. They will generally be of several types:

▶ *Situational.* You will be given a scenario and asked to select the appropriate response.

▶ *Definitional.* You will be asked to identify the meaning of a word, term, or phrase.

▶ *Fill in the blank.* You will be given an incomplete sentence and have to select the answer that completes it. Be aware that the correct answer may seem grammatically awkward due to tense or number.

▶ *Computations.* You will be given data and be expected to produce the correct mathematical answer. For example, you may have questions about PERT that require calculations.

▶ *Data interpretation.* It is not unusual to be given a table of values and be asked to calculate various earned value indicators.

▶ Other types that may arise.

Test-Taking Tips

1. There is no penalty for guessing. Leaving an answer blank guarantees that you will get it wrong! Eliminate the obvious incorrect choices to improve your odds.

2. The minute you are released to begin the test, write down all of the formulas that you might need. Generally these will relate to earned value, PERT scheduling, and financial indicators from the cost knowledge area. This has two advantages. First, you can concentrate on other questions,

and second, you will be less anxious about the calculations when you see them.

3. Take the day before the exam off. Do not study, and try to avoid working long hours or on controversial subjects. We all remember "cramming" the night before finals, and how ineffective it was. The PMP is not a "crammable" exam; it is based on knowledge and experience.

4. Do not agonize over a question that you unsure of. Mark it for later review. Perhaps a subsequent question will help you with the answer.

5. Absolutes such as "always" and "never" are supposed to have been purged from the question bank. However, one could still turn up. Absolutes are almost never the right choice!

6. Many questions may be answered incorrectly because you did not read the question *and* all four answers thoroughly. One of the early choices may seem correct, but a later choice will be the right answer.

7. Remember to answer the questions from PMI's perspective. You may not agree, but it is their exam and they hold all of the cards. Review the section on decomposition of the WBS to see an example: PMI says level of effort is done in scheduling, although many others maintain that it is done in scope. Answer PMI's way.

8. When studying earned value analysis, memorize the formulas and tips that I wrote about in Chapter 7 on cost management. Remember that PMI uses PV, EV, and AC, not BCWS, BCWP, and ACWP.

9. Remember other PMIisms, such as historical information, a WBS must be used for everything, no gold plating, project managers wear white hats and must seek out the truth, and not be passive, everyone must be involved in decisions, stakeholders rule, and other recurring themes from the PMBOK.

10. Think long and hard before you change an answer. If another question has given you insight, fine, but many correct answers are changed needlessly.

KEEPING YOUR CERTIFICATION

Even though you don't have it yet, PMI requires continuing education to keep your PMP certification. You must accumulate Professional Development Units (PDUs) in a variety of ways. These are spelled out on the Web site and will also be in the credentials packet that you will receive from PMI.

You need to obtain 60 PDUs every three years. This is not difficult if you take courses to maintain your proficiency. Most courses you will take grant Continuing Education Units (CEUs), and PMI has a conversion table on their Web site. All PDU reporting activity is done via the Internet.

Another way to get PDUs is through presentations to your local chapter. I recommend this method for a variety of reasons, not the least of which is that it makes you stand up in front of a crowd and present something! What better training for presenting your project to the board of directors of your company?

CONCLUSION

This chapter does not have an "Areas of Emphasis" or "Sample Questions." It does have a conclusion, however. That conclusion is that we hope you have found the material useful and entertaining. No single source can prepare you for the exam, but having read this book and taken the practice exams will have prepared you well for success.

Good luck, and welcome to the ranks of Project Management Professionals!

Appendix

Answers to Chapter Questions

CHAPTER 2 ANSWERS

Project Management Context	
1	C
2	D
3	B
4	A
5	C
6	B
7	A
8	C
9	D
10	D
11	B
12	C
13	A
14	B
15	D
16	C
17	B
18	D
19	D
20	A

CHAPTER 3 ANSWERS

Project Management Processes	
1	A
2	B
3	B
4	C
5	D
6	D
7	B
8	A
9	C
10	D

CHAPTER 4 ANSWERS

Project Integration Management	
1	D
2	B
3	C
4	C
5	A
6	A
7	C
8	B
9	C
10	B
11	C
12	A
13	C
14	D

15	B
16	D
17	A
18	C
19	D
20	B

CHAPTER 5 ANSWERS

Scope Management	
1	B
2	D
3	C
4	C
5	B
6	A
7	C
8	C
9	D
10	B
11	A
12	D
13	A
14	B
15	D
16	B
17	A
18	D
19	B
20	A

CHAPTER 6 ANSWERS

Time Management	
1	C
2	B
3	D
4	B
5	A
6	D
7	C
8	D
9	A
10	C
11	A
12	B
13	C
14	B
15	D
16	B
17	D
18	C
19	D
20	B

CHAPTER 7 ANSWERS

Cost Management	
1	D
2	B
3	A
4	C

5	C
6	A
7	C
8	C
9	A
10	A
11	A
12	C
13	B
14	D
15	C
16	B
17	A
18	D
19	C
20	D

CHAPTER 8 ANSWERS

Quality Management	
1	D
2	A
3	C
4	B
5	B
6	C
7	A
8	C
9	C
10	A

CHAPTER 8 ANSWERS *Continued*

11	B
12	D
13	D
14	A
15	C
16	A
17	B
18	D
19	C
20	B

CHAPTER 9 ANSWERS

Human Resources Answers	
1	C
2	C
3	B
4	A
5	D
6	C
7	A
8	C
9	B
10	C
11	B
12	D
13	C
14	A
15	C

CHAPTER 10 ANSWERS

Project Communications Questions	
1	C
2	D
3	A
4	B
5	D
6	C
7	D
8	A
9	B
10	A

CHAPTER 11 ANSWERS

Risk	
1	C
2	B
3	A
4	D
5	B
6	B
7	D
8	B
9	C
10	B
11	B
12	C
13	B
14	D

CHAPTER 11 ANSWERS *Continued*

15	A
16	A
17	C
18	C
19	D
20	C

CHAPTER 12 ANSWERS

Procurement	
1	D
2	D
3	B
4	C
5	A
6	D
7	B
8	C
9	B
10	C
11	D
12	B
13	A
14	C
15	D
16	C
17	D
18	B
19	C
20	D

CHAPTER 13 ANSWERS

Professional Responsibility	
1	A
2	B
3	C
4	B
5	A
6	D
7	D
8	C
9	D
10	D

References and Reading List

Archibald, R. D., and R. L. Villoria. *Network-Based Management Systems (PERT/CPM)*. New York: Wiley, 1967.

Brooks, F. P. *The Mythical Man-Month: Essays on Software Engineering*. Reading, MA: Addison-Wesley, 1975.

Chen, Yanping, and Francis N. Arko. *Principles of Contracting for Project Management*. Arlington, VA: UMT Press, 2003

Cialdini, Robert B. *Influence: The Power of Persuasion,* Revised Edition. New York: Quill, 1993.

Cleland, David I., and William R. King, Editors. *Project Management Handbook*. New York: Van Nostrand Reinhold, 1983.

Fleming, Quentin W., and Joel M. Koppelman. *Earned Value Project Management*. Upper Darby, PA: Project Management Institute, 1996.

Frame, J. Davidson. *Managing Projects in Organizations*. San Francisco: Jossey-Bass, 1995.

Frame, J. Davidson. *The New Project Management,* 2d ed. San Francisco: Jossey-Bass, 2002.

Frame, J. Davidson. *Project Finance: Tools and Techniques*. Arlington, VA: UMT Press, 2003.

Gause, Donald, and Gerald Weinberg. *Exploring Requirements: Quality Before Design.* New York: Dorset House Publishing, 1989.

Goldratt, Eliyahu M. *Critical Chain.* Great Barrington, MA: The North River Press, 1997.

Graham, Robert J., and Randall L. Englund. *Creating an Environment for Successful Projects.* San Francisco: Jossey-Bass, 1997.

Kerzner, Harold. *In Search of Excellence in Project Management.* New York: Van Nostrand, 1998.

Kerzner, Harold. *Project Management: A Systems Approach to Planning, Scheduling, and Controlling,* 5th ed. New York: Van Nostrand, 1995.

Lewis, James. *Fundamentals of Project Management,* 2d ed. New York: AMACOM, 2001.

———. *Mastering Project Management.* New York: McGraw-Hill, 1998.

———. *Project Leadership.* New York: McGraw-Hill, 2002.

———. *Project Planning, Scheduling and Control,* 3d ed. New York: McGraw-Hill, 2000.

———. *The Project Manager's Desk Reference,* 2d ed. New York: McGraw-Hill, 2000.

———. *The Project Manager's Pocket Survival Guide.* New York: McGraw-Hill, 2003.

———. *Team-Based Project Management.* New York: AMACOM, 1997.

———. *Working Together.* New York: McGraw-Hill, 2002.

Moder, Joseph J., Cecil R. Phillips, and Edward W. Davis. *Project Management with CPM, PERT, and Precedence Diagramming,* 3d ed. New York: Van Nostrand, 1983.

Pinto, Jeffrey K. *Power and Politics in Project Management.* Upper Darby, PA: Project Management Institute, 1996.

Pinto, Jeffrey K., Editor. *The Project Management Institute Project Management Handbook.* San Francisco: Jossey-Bass, 1998.

Sugimoto, T. *Estimation on the Project Management Workload.* In "Proceedings of the International Conference on Project Management," Singapore, 31 July to 2 August, 2002.

Wysocki, Robert K. *Effective Project Management,* 2d ed. New York: Wiley, 2000.

Wysocki, Robert K, and James P. Lewis. *The World-Class Project Manager.* Boston: Perseus Books, 2000.

Index

About the Authors

James P. Lewis, Ph.D., PMP, is president of The Lewis Institute, Inc., a project management training and consulting company. Lewis wrote *The Project Manager's Desk Reference, Project Planning, Scheduling, and Control,* and a number of other project management titles.

Robert E. Dudley, PMP, teaches project management at the University of Wisconsin School of Executive Education and is the president of Kenilworth Project Services.